A
SPIRITUAL
HERITAGE

TOUR OF THE UNITED STATES CAPITOL

Aledo, Texas
www.wallbuilders.com

A SELF-GUIDED TOUR

DAVID BARTON

A Spiritual Heritage Tour of the United States Capitol
Copyright © 2000, David Barton
2nd edition, 2nd printing

Additional materials available from:
WallBuilders
P. O. Box 397
Aledo, Texas 76008
(817) 441-6044
www.wallbuilders.com

Cover Design:
Jeremiah Pent
Lincoln-Jackson
235 Wenner Way
Ft. Washington, PA 19034

ISBN-10: 0-925279-71-4
ISBN-13: 978-0-925279-71-2

Printed in the United States of America

Table of Contents

A Spiritual Heritage Tour
of the United States Capitol

A Spiritual Heritage Tour of the United States Capitol

The Capitol building of the United States of America – what a majestic edifice! This is one of a very few structures recognized the world over. In virtually any land, whoever sees a picture of this building knows it is the American seat of government!

This grand structure has been the scene of some of the most profound moments in America's history. In its two centuries of use, this building has welcomed the voices of some of our greatest heroes, has survived some of America's most desperate and foreboding dangers, and has witnessed important decisions affecting American life and culture.

Truly, many diverse stories record the heritage of this building. There are stories reflecting its architectural heritage, its political heritage, and its artistic heritage, but especially interesting are the stories reflecting its rich spiritual heritage. Because the spiritual heritage within this building is little known by most Americans today, this tour through the United States Capitol will highlight many of the stories and artifacts within the Capitol that confirm the deep roots of religious faith throughout American public life.

THE ROTUNDA

We will begin in the Rotunda. The Rotunda is in the center of the Capitol, and its entry is on the second floor. (Included in Appendix A is the floor plan of the interior of the Capitol, showing its rooms and floors. Please refer to the floor plan as the various rooms are discussed throughout this book.) The free-standing dome of the Rotunda is so tall that the Statue of Liberty could be placed inside and there would still be nearly 30 feet left above her torch!

When Congress first moved into the Capitol in 1800, the building bore little resemblance to the current one. In the mid-1820s the Rotunda was completed, and not until 1863 was the massive dome built atop the Rotunda. It required nearly 70 years of construction for the Capitol to become the familiar structure we recognize today.

THE CAPITOL IN 1800

THE CAPITOL IN 1807. THE ORIGINAL CAPITOL (THE LEFT HALF) BECAME THE SENATE CHAMBERS. A WOODEN WALKWAY CONNECTED IT TO THE NEW HOUSE CHAMBERS (THE RIGHT HALF).

THE CAPITOL IN 1814 AFTER IT WAS BURNED BY THE BRITISH

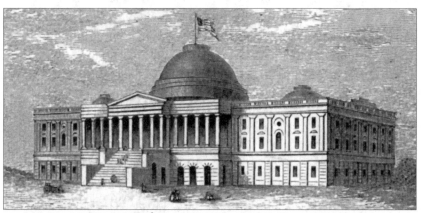

THE CAPITOL IN THE 1820S AFTER THE COMPLETION OF THE ROTUNDA

THE CAPITOL IN THE 1850S AFTER THE ADDITION OF THE
HOUSE & SENATE WING EXTENSIONS

THE CAPITOL IN THE 1860S AFTER THE ADDITION OF THE DOME

When the Rotunda opened to the public in 1824, the first things to catch the eye – both then and now – were the massive oil paintings which adorn the walls of the Rotunda. There are eight paintings; each measures 14 feet by 20 feet; and each depicts an important event bearing on our history.

The four pictures on the east side depict the age of Exploration and Colonization; they were placed in the Rotunda between 1840 and 1855. The first is of Columbus landing in the Western World in 1492, depicting the prayer service held following his landing; the second is of DeSoto discovering the Mississippi River in 1541; the third is of the baptism of Pocahontas at Jamestown, Virginia, in 1613; and the fourth is of the Pilgrims in 1620, praying before departing from Holland to America. (Already, in just these four pictures, there are two prayer meetings and a baptism – an early indicator of the religious heritage found throughout the building.)

The four paintings on the west side of the Rotunda were all in place in 1824 when the Rotunda originally opened; each represents an important event in America's quest for independence. They include the Signing of the Declaration of Independence in 1776; the Battle of Saratoga in 1777 (America's first major victory of the American Revolution); the Victory at Yorktown in 1781 (the last battle of the American Revolution); and George Washington resigning as Commander-in-Chief of the Continental Army in 1783.

PICTURES IN THE ROTUNDA

THE LANDING OF COLUMBUS IN 1492

DISCOVERY OF THE MISSISSIPPI IN 1541

PICTURES IN THE ROTUNDA

THE BAPTISM OF POCAHONTAS IN 1613

THE EMBARKATION OF THE PILGRIMS IN 1620

PICTURES IN THE ROTUNDA

THE DECLARATION OF INDEPENDENCE IN 1776

SURRENDER OF GENERAL BURGOYNE AT SARATOGA IN 1777

PICTURES IN THE ROTUNDA

THE SURRENDER OF CORNWALLIS AT YORKTOWN IN 1781

GENERAL GEORGE WASHINGTON RESIGNING HIS COMMISSION IN 1783

In addition to these eight pictures, several statues of America's heroes and statesmen line the walls of the Rotunda. Each of the fifty States is allowed to display two statues of individuals from that State within the Capitol. (There are also five to ten other statues here, depending on various displays at any given time.) So, if an individual is commemorated by a statue in the Capitol, it is indeed a great honor – very few individuals from across America's long history have ever been accorded this distinction.

Most of the statues began arriving at the Capitol in 1870 and are found primarily in four rooms: the Rotunda, East Central Hall, the Hall of Columns, and National Statuary Hall (refer to Appendix A). Although the statues are occasionally shuffled around to different locations within the Capitol or sometimes replaced by a different statue from the State (as in the case of an astronaut from Colorado), such changes do not happen often. For the most part, the statues are generally of earlier leaders and statesmen and generally remain in the same area.

Many of the statues and paintings within the Capitol will be highlighted as individual rooms are examined. Let's start, however, by focusing our attention on the events depicted in the eight paintings in the Rotunda, beginning with the Embarkation of the Pilgrims in 1620 (see picture on page 10). The Pilgrims are kneeling in prayer, committing their endeavor to God. Notice especially the Bible in the center of the picture around which they are gathered. That Bible is a "Geneva Bible."

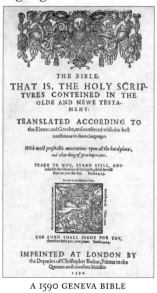

A 1590 GENEVA BIBLE

The Geneva Bible (140 editions were printed from 1560 to 1644 [1]) was the favorite of those who were called Pilgrims, Separatists, Dissenters, and Puritans. [2] These groups believed that there was much corruption in the organized church of the sixteenth century and that many of the church's practices had become anti-Biblical; they objected to those corrupt practices (hence the title "Dissenters"). Some "dissenters" dedicated themselves completely unto God and separated themselves from the church and its objectionable practices (and consequently were called "Separatists") while other "dissenters" sought to cleanse and purify the church from within (and thus were called "Puritans").

The Geneva Bible was the Bible that the early religious colonists (often called "Pilgrims") brought to America's shores. This Bible, despite its size of nearly 6 inches by 8 inches, was called a "pocket" Bible. (Previous editions of the Bible were huge and unwieldy, some being over two feet in height!) Many of the earlier Bibles were termed "Pulpit Bibles" because they were, in fact, often chained to the pulpits of churches. However, with the Geneva Bible, a person could individually possess and also read the Word of God without having to rely on a king or church official to interpret what the Bible said.

THE FIRST EPISTLE OF PAVL TO TIMOTHEVS.

COMMENTARIES BY REFORMATION LEADERS FILLED THE MARGINS OF THE GENEVA BIBLE

The most unique feature of the Geneva Bible – and the feature which so impacted American culture – was its marginal commentaries. These commentaries were largely the work of reformers who had been driven from Great Britain during the reigns of Bloody Mary and James I – two monarchs who were advocates of the Divine Right of Kings and of the authority of the State over the Church. The commentaries in the Geneva Bible reflected reformation thought and took an anti-autocratic tone toward both church leaders and state leaders.

With such open criticism of church and state leaders, the Pilgrims became the target of harsh religious and government persecution. Seeking a place where they could serve God according to their interpretation of the Scriptures, the Pilgrims arrived in America in November 1620. While still anchored offshore, the Pilgrims estab-

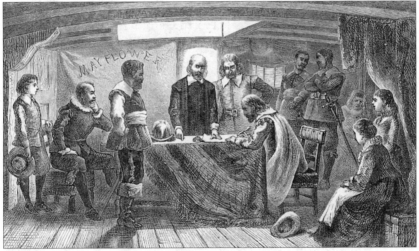

SIGNING THE MAYFLOWER COMPACT

lished the "Mayflower Compact" – the first government document written on this continent.

The "Mayflower Compact" articulated two important Biblical principles emphasized in the Geneva commentaries. The first was that of evangelization, and thus the Pilgrims declared that they had come to this continent for the express purpose of evangelizing the nation to a knowledge of Jesus Christ. The second religious principle in that document was what is now termed social compact – that individuals knit themselves together into a community which would then govern itself under fixed standards. In the case of the Pilgrims, their fixed standards were those established in God's Word.

The small seeds of social compact, local control, and community self-government introduced into America by the religious immigrants pictured in the Rotunda took root and grew. A century-and-a-half later, those seeds were brought to maturity when our Founding Fathers announced those same principles in the Declaration of Independence – including the principle that all of America would now govern itself under God's laws: "the laws of nature and of nature's God."

So strong was their reliance on God's Word and precepts during the American Revolution that even the currency and flags reflected this

CURRENCY OF THE REVOLUTION

reliance. For example, the emblem on North Carolina's currency contained the words "The law is our king" emblazoned upon an open Bible, and several revolutionary flags and banners openly appealed to God. Unquestionably, during the American Revolution, the Bible and God's law were *officially* recognized as the basis of American self-government – the concept introduced a century-and-a-half earlier by the Pilgrims.

FLAGS OF THE REVOLUTION

However, the Pilgrims were responsible for introducing more into America than just the concept of self-government based on God's standards. They also introduced from the Bible many ideas that have become established parts of our culture today, including free-enterprise, the hard-work ethic, workfare rather than welfare, and private property ownership. [3]

It is understandable that the Geneva Bible – particularly with its anti-autocratic commentaries – would be seen as a problem by the rulers of that day. In reaction, supporters of autocracy published the Bishops'

Bible and the Rheims Bible, both of which specifically attacked the content of the Geneva commentaries. [4] This type of conflict was a factor leading to the establishment of official versions of the Bible. [5]

In probably the best-known example, King James I of England authorized the funding of a new translation of the Bible about 1600, and it was finally published in 1611. Even though it was translated from essentially the same manuscripts as the Geneva Bible, this version removed all the commentaries and thus silenced the dissenting voice.

THE 1611 KING JAMES VERSION (LEFT) ELIMINATED THE REFORMATON COMMENTARIES FOUND IN THE GENEVA BIBLE (RIGHT)

Not surprisingly, then, the "authorized" or King James Bible became the official Bible of many British monarchs and was therefore often the official Bible of the English colonies. In fact, Great Britain even made it illegal for the British colonies to print a Bible in the English language. [6] By this stipulation, all English-language Bibles were to be printed under the supervision of the Crown, thus helping regulate which versions were in circulation. (This law will be significant in a later discussion of the paintings in the Rotunda from the Revolutionary era.)

There is one other painting in the Rotunda in which the Geneva Bible had a direct influence: the Baptism of Pocahontas. Pocahontas was one of the first converts to Christianity in the New World (led to Christ by John Rolfe, who later became her husband), and the Geneva Bible was apparently influential in her conversion. The picture depicts Pocahontas being baptized in 1613 by the Rev. Alexander Whitaker (see page 10). Interestingly, on her baptism, Pocahontas changed her name to Rebecka, wanting a Biblical name to accompany her through her new life.

POCAHONTAS AS "REBECKA"

Turning to the west side of the Rotunda, the four paintings there focus on the American Revolution, moving forward some 150 years beyond the Age of Discovery and Colonization. These four were painted by one of our Founding Fathers: John Trumbull, "The Painter of the Revolution."

JOHN TRUMBULL, "THE PAINTER OF THE REVOLUTION"

John Trumbull served as an officer during the American Revolution, and what makes his paintings so meaningful is that he personally witnessed much of what he painted and personally knew many of those whom he painted in the pictures. Because of his commitment to artistic accuracy, the faces in his paintings in the Rotunda are probably about as close as is possible to having photographs of our Founding Fathers.

John Trumbull came from a family of outspoken Christians, and other members of his family are also honored in the Capitol. For example, his brother Jonathan, who was a colonel during the Revolution as well as an officer on George Washington's staff, is included in the painting of the surrender of Lord Cornwallis at Yorktown.

After the Revolution, Jonathan became Governor of Connecticut; and while

COLONEL JONATHAN TRUMBULL

Governor, he issued several proclamations – with strong evangelical language – calling his entire State to extended times of prayer. It is

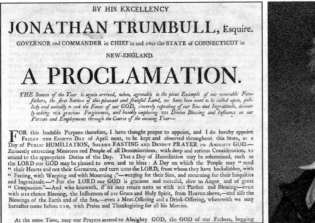

not surprising, however, that he issued such evangelical proclamations, for they reflect his very nature. In fact, Jonathan Trumbull was one among the overwhelming majority of our Founding Fathers and early leaders who were strongly and openly religious.

There are many today who dispute this fact. Rather than acknowledge that Christianity played an important role in the formation of this nation, or that there is a deep and rich religious heritage attached to the Capitol building, or that most of our Founding Fathers were strongly and openly religious, they instead claim just the opposite. For example, one prominent historian amazingly asserts, "The Founding Fathers were at most deists." [7] And in an article entitled "America's UnChristian Beginnings," the writer forcefully claims that "The early presidents and patriots were generally deists or Unitarians, believing in some form of impersonal Providence but rejecting the divinity of Jesus and the relevance of the Bible." [8] Another author similarly charges, "[M]ost of our other patriarchs were at best deists, [not] believing in . . . the God of the Old and New Testaments." [9] And the title of one book seems to say it all: *The Godless Constitution.* [10]

The reason that such absurd accusations often go unrefuted by the average citizen is that most Americans don't know who our Founders were. For example, in the picture of the signing of the Constitution (this picture will be discussed in detail later in a different room in the Capitol) how many of the 39 signers can the average citizen identify?

THE SIGNING OF THE CONSTITUTION

Which one is Gouverneur Morris? Or William Paterson? Or John Dickinson? Although each of these signers played crucial roles, most Americans today have never heard of them. Similarly, in the picture of the signers of the Declaration (see page 11), which one is Stephen Hopkins? Or Samuel Huntington? Or Richard Henry Lee? If citizens don't know who our Founders were, then they clearly can't address the question of whether or not they were religious.

In earlier years, charges of the non-religious nature of our Founders were immediately dismissed because citizens knew about our individual Founders. For example, the textbook from 1848 pictured on the right [11] (recently reprinted), was used in classrooms for decades. It provided

1848 SCHOOL BOOK

a brief biography of *each* of the 56 signers of the Declaration and was quite candid about the strong Christian faith of so many of them.

In a return to the practice of these earlier schoolbooks, let's examine some of the religious beliefs held by Founders depicted, for example, in the painting of the signing of the Declaration of Independence.

Realize that every individual in the painting had an impact on the Declaration of Independence, even though not everyone pictured actually signed it. Why? Because even though Congress approved the Declaration on July 4th, 1776, it was then signed only by the President and Secretary of Congress. The final engrossed version of the Declaration was not signed by most representatives until August 2nd; and during that intervening month, some who had voted for the Declaration were called away to the service of their country before they could sign.

For example, George Clinton voted for the final draft of the Declaration on July 4th, but before he could sign, he was called to assume military leadership in New York. And even though Robert Livingston was on the five-man committee charged with writing the Declaration, he was recalled to serve in his State legislature before he could sign the very document he had helped draft. George Clinton and Robert Livingston, even though they ultimately did not sign the Declaration, are both in the Rotunda painting of the signing of the Declaration and each is so significant that he has been honored with a statue at the Capitol.

CLINTON (LEFT) & LIVINGSTON (RIGHT) BOTH APPROVED THE DECLARATION BUT WERE UNABLE TO SIGN IT

On the other hand, some of those who signed the final version of the Declaration had not been in Congress on July 4th to vote for it, including Benjamin Rush and George Clymer. So, every individual in the painting, either by voting or by signing, in some significant way contributed to the Declaration of Independence. Now, what of their religious beliefs?

RUSH (LEFT) AND
CLYMER (RIGHT)

• • • •

A GUIDE TO IDENTIFYING SIGNERS OF THE DECLARATION

1. GEORGE WYTHE, VA
2. WILLIAM WHIPPLE, NH
3. JOSIAH BARTLETT, NH
4. THOMAS LYNCH, SC
5. BENJAMIN HARRISON, VA
6. RICHARD HENRY LEE, VA
7. SAMUEL ADAMS, MA
8. GEORGE CLINTON, NY *
9. WILLIAM PACA, MD
10. SAMUEL CHASE, MD
11. LEWIS MORRIS, NY
12. WILLIAM FLOYD, NY
13. ARTHUR MIDDLETON, SC
14. THOMAS HEYWARD, JR., SC
15. CHARLES CARROLL, MD
16. GEORGE WALTON, GA

17. ROBERT MORRIS, PA
18. THOMAS WILLING, PA *
19. BENJAMIN RUSH, PA
20. ELBRIDGE GERRY, MA
21. ROBERT TREAT PAINE, MA
22. ABRAHAM CLARK, NJ
23. STEPHEN HOPKINS, RI
24. WILLIAM ELLERY, RI
25. GEORGE CLYMER, PA
26. WILLIAM HOOPER, NC
27. JOSEPH HEWES, NC
28. JAMES WILSON, PA
29. FRANCIS HOPKINSON, NJ
30. JOHN ADAMS, MA
31. ROGER SHERMAN, CT
32. ROBERT LIVINGSTON, NY *

33. THOMAS JEFFERSON, VA
34. BENJAMIN FRANKLIN, PA
35. RICHARD STOCKTON, NJ
36. FRANCIS LEWIS, NY
37. JOHN WITHERSPOON, NJ
38. SAMUEL HUNTINGTON, CT
39. WILLIAM WILLIAMS, CT
40. OLIVER WOLCOTT, CT
41. JOHN HANCOCK, MA
42. CHARLES THOMSON, PA *
43. GEORGE READ, DE
44. JOHN DICKINSON, PA *
45. EDWARD RUTLEDGE, SC
46. THOMAS MCKEAN, DE
47. PHILIP LIVINGSTON, NY

* THE 5 MEN WHOSE NAMES ARE STARRED WERE NOT SIGNERS, BUT DID HAVE A SIGNIFICANT IMPACT ON THE CREATION OF THE DECLARATION OF INDEPENDENCE.

THERE WERE 56 SIGNERS OF THE DECLARATION. THE PORTRAITS OF THE FOLLOWING 14 SIGNERS DO NOT APPEAR IN THE PAINTING.

MATTHEW THORNTON, NH
JOHN HART, NJ
JOHN MORTON, PA
JAMES SMITH, PA
GEORGE TAYLOR, PA

GEORGE ROSS, PA
CAESAR RODNEY, DE
THOMAS STONE, MD
THOMAS NELSON, JR., VA
FRANCIS LIGHTFOOT LEE, VA

CARTER BRAXTON, VA
JOHN PENN, NC
BUTTON GWINNETT, GA
LYMAN HALL, GA

Begin with John Witherspoon. He was an ordained minister of the Gospel, published several books of Gospel sermons, and played major roles in two American editions of the Bible, including one from 1791 that is considered America's first family Bible.

The Rev. Dr. Witherspoon wrote the introduction for this Bible, and although the Bible's text is essentially the same as that of the King James version, it does not carry that title. After all, the Americans – including Dr. Witherspoon – had just fought a war to be free of kings, so why attach the name of a king to an American edition of the Bible? Therefore, this Bible describes itself only as "The Holy Bible" because, as Dr. Witherspoon pointed out, this was *God's* Word, not the word of a king! [12]

John Witherspoon, signer of the Declaration and minister of the Gospel, helped produce America's very first family Bible.

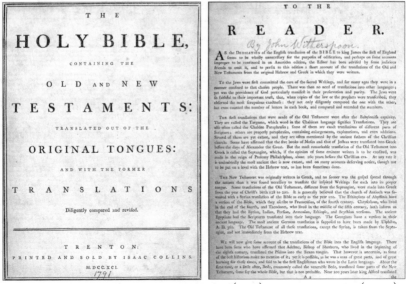

THE 1791 BIBLE PREPARED BY DR. WITHERSPOON (LEFT), HIS INTRODUCTION (RIGHT), AND ONE OF HIS MANY BOOKS OF SERMONS (UPPER LEFT)

Consider next Charles Thomson. Charles Thomson was the Secretary of Congress,

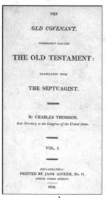

and he and John Hancock were the only two to sign the first draft of the Declaration of Independence. Charles Thomson is another Founder responsible for

THOMSON'S BIBLE

an American edition of the Bible. That Bible – called Thomson's Bible – was the first translation of the Greek Septuagint into English. It took Charles Thomson twenty-five years to complete his translation, but even today that work is still considered one of the more scholarly American translations of the Bible.

Consider also signer Charles Carroll of Carrollton. Charles Carroll was the last of the fifty-six signers to pass away, dying in 1832 at the age of 95. A strong and unequivocal declaration of his Christian faith appears in numerous writings, including a letter he wrote on his 89th birthday in which he declared: "On the mercy of my Redeemer I rely for salvation, and on His merits; not on the works I have done in obedience to His precepts." [13] In other of his writings, Charles Carroll explained that his Christian faith was one of the chief reasons that he had entered

CARROLL'S LETTER EXPRESSING HIS
STRONG CHRISTIAN FAITH

OF THE UNITED STATES CAPITOL

into the American Revolution – he was fighting to preserve religious liberty. In fact, he was so committed to Christianity that he built and personally funded a Christian house of worship. [14]

CHARLES CARROLL

Charles Carroll's life and words confirm that he was a strong Christian, and he is one of that handful of Americans who have been honored at the Capitol with a statue, located in East Central Hall.

Consider next signer Benjamin Rush. When he

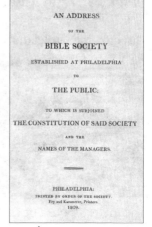

died in 1813, the writings of the day, and the other Founders who were still alive, declared that Dr. Rush was one of our three most notable Founders, ranking him in prominence along with George Washington and Benjamin Franklin. [15] Yet who today has heard of Benjamin Rush, or who knows of his accomplishments?

Benjamin Rush was a leading educator, helping start five colleges and universities, including the first college for women. Additionally, he is called the "Father of American Medicine," personally trained three thousand students for their medical degrees, published a number of medical textbooks, and made numerous medical discoveries which still benefit us today. He was also a founder of America's first abolition society and for forty years was a national leader in the abolition movement.

Because of his faith, we still enjoy the fruit of his labors. For example, in 1791, Dr. Rush founded "The First Day Society" which grew into today's Sunday Schools. Additionally, he also started America's first Bible society: The Bible Society of Philadelphia. The original constitution for that Bible society was authored by Dr. Rush.

AN ADDRESS

OF THE

BIBLE SOCIETY

ESTABLISHED AT PHILADELPHIA

TO

THE PUBLIC;

TO WHICH IS SUBJOINED

THE CONSTITUTION OF SAID SOCIETY

AND THE

NAMES OF THE MANAGERS.

PHILADELPHIA:
PRINTED BY ORDER OF THE SOCIETY.
Fry and Kammerer, Printers.
1809.

DR. RUSH'S BIBLE SOCIETY ADDRESS

In that constitution, Dr. Rush listed two important reasons that America needed Bible societies: first, he pointed out that with a Bible, every individual could discover how to have a personal relationship with God through Jesus Christ; second, he argued that if every individual owned a Bible – and would study and obey it – that all of our social problems, including crime, slavery, etc., would diminish. As Dr. Rush explained, it is in living by the Bible that man becomes both "humanized and civilized." [16]

In looking for ways to print Bibles faster and more economically, Dr. Rush and the Society came across what was called stereotyped printing – an early form of mass production. With the help of President James Madison and an act passed by Congress in the Capitol building, [17] Dr. Rush's Bible society obtained stereotype plates by which they could mass produce Bibles. The result was America's first mass-produced, stereotyped Bible – and it came about through the efforts

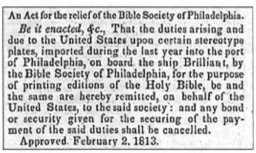

An Act for the relief of the Bible Society of Philadelphia.

Be it enacted, &c., That the duties arising and due to the United States upon certain stereotype plates, imported during the last year into the port of Philadelphia, on board the ship Brilliant, by the Bible Society of Philadelphia, for the purpose of printing editions of the Holy Bible, be and the same are hereby remitted, on behalf of the United States, to the said society: and any bond or security given for the securing of the payment of the said duties shall be cancelled. Approved. February 2, 1813.

THE CONGRESSIONAL ACT THAT AIDED THE BIBLE SOCIETY

of Dr. Benjamin Rush, signer of the Declaration of Independence.

Consider next signer Francis Hopkinson. He was a church music director, a choir leader, and the editor of a music work from 1767 – one

of the first hymnals printed in America. His work took the one hundred and fifty Psalms and set them all to music so that the Psalms could be sung much as King David had done over two thousand years before. Interestingly, his work was one of the earliest in America to include musical notation and place notes in a staff so that the melody could be seen. This unique Bible hymnbook was the work of Declaration signer, Francis Hopkinson.

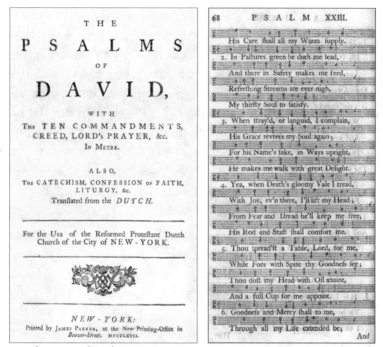

HOPKINSON'S HYMNAL (LEFT) AND THE TWENTY-THIRD PSALM FROM THAT HYMNAL (RIGHT)

Consider also signer Richard Stockton. Like the others of the signers, he pledged his life, fortune, and sacred honor for the cause of American

independence; and like the others, he kept his promise. In fact, he was one of nine signers of the Declaration who did not survive the American Revolution.

Richard Stockton was captured by the British and, as an American prisoner of war, was tortured and severely abused. Incidentally, during the American Revolution, it was actually safer for an American soldier to be on the battlefield facing British muskets than to be captured and placed in a British prisoner of war camp. Thousands more Americans died from British prisoner of war camps than from British bullets. [18]

The Americans eventually were able to arrange for the release of Richard Stockton through a prisoner exchange; but his health was so crushed that he never recovered; he was dying and he knew it. Understanding this, he placed his temporal affairs in order and penned his last will and testament. Notice his strong Christian faith evident in that document:

[A]s my children will have frequent occasion of perusing this instrument, and may probably be particularly impressed with the last words of their father, I think it proper here not only to subscribe to the entire belief of the great and leading doctrines of the Christian religion, such as the being of God;

the universal defection and depravity of human nature; the Divinity of the person and the completeness of the redemption purchased by the blessed Savior; the necessity of the operations of the Divine Spirit; of Divine faith accompanied with an habitual virtuous life; and the universality of the Divine Providence: but also, in the bowels of a father's affection, to exhort and charge [my children] that the fear of God is the beginning of wisdom, that the way of life held up in the Christian system is calculated for the most complete happiness that can be enjoyed in this mortal state, [and] that all occasions of vice and immorality is injurious either immediately or consequentially – even in this life. [19]

RICHARD STOCKTON

There is no doubt that this Founding Father – who sacrificed his life for our freedom – was a strong Christian; and he has been honored in the Capitol with a statue, located in East Central Hall.

Consider also signer Thomas McKean.  He was one of America's leading legal authorities and was responsible for a 1792 *Commentaries on the Constitution of the United States of America.* Thomas McKean, in addition to signing the Declaration of Independence, also helped author the constitutions of Pennsylvania and of Delaware and served as governor in each of those States. Additionally, he was the Chief Justice of the Supreme Court of Pennsylvania.

In the case *Republica v. John Roberts* [20] (a trial over which Chief Justice McKean presided), John Roberts was sentenced to death after a jury found him guilty of treason. (In those days, a sentence of death meant that the prisoner had just a few days left on earth, not fifteen to twenty years.) After reporting the jury's decision and delivering the sentence, Chief Justice McKean then offered these words of wisdom to John Roberts:

MCKEAN'S *COMMENTARIES*

You will probably have but a short time to live. Before you launch into eternity, it behooves you to improve the time that may be allowed you in this world: it behooves you most seriously to reflect upon your past conduct; to repent of your evil deeds; to be incessant in prayers to the great and merciful God to forgive your manifold transgressions and sins; to teach you to rely upon the merit and passion of a dear Redeemer, and thereby to avoid those regions of sorrow – those doleful shades where peace and rest can never dwell, where even hope cannot enter. It behooves you to seek the [fellowship], advice, and prayers of pious and good men; to be [persistent] at the Throne of Grace, and to learn the way that leadeth to happiness. May you, reflecting upon these things, and pursuing the will of the great Father of light and life, be received into [the] company and society of angels and archangels and the spirits of just men made perfect; and may you be qualified to enter into the joys of Heaven – joys unspeakable and full of glory! [21]

If one accepts the current ridiculous charges that our Founders were not religious, then this is the account of an alleged deist Founding Father giving a very Christ-centered altar call in a courtroom. Hardly! Signer of the Declaration Thomas McKean was another of our many Founding Fathers who was a strong Christian.

Consider next signer John Hancock. After serving as a President of Congress during the Revolution, he was elected Governor of Massachusetts, where he issued several proclamations calling the citizens to prayer, fasting, and thanksgiving. Hancock's proclamation

from October 15, 1791, is typical of his others: it contains strongly evangelical language.

For example, notice the request with which he closes that proclamation: And pray especially "that universal happiness may be established in the world; [and] that all may bow to the scepter of our Lord Jesus Christ, and the whole earth be filled with His glory." [22] John Hancock also issued other religious proclamations, each equally evangelical in nature,

ONE OF HANCOCK'S
MANY PROCLAMATIONS

and all fully reflective of his own Christian beliefs.

John Hancock is another of our Founders who was open about his faith and who has been honored with a statue at the Capitol, located in the east corridor of the Senate wing.

JOHN HANCOCK

Consider signer Samuel Adams. Because of his leadership in events like the Boston Tea Party and organizations such as the Sons of Liberty, he has been titled "The Father of the American Revolution." After the Revolution, Samuel Adams remained very active in political affairs. For example, he was one of the individuals responsible for the movement that led to the drafting and adoption of the Bill of Rights, and he later became the Lieutenant Governor and then Governor of Massachusetts.

As governor, he, like John Hancock, issued several proclamations for prayer, fasting, and thanksgiving which used strong evangelical language. For example, in his 1795 proclamation, Adams closed by asking citizens to pray "that the peaceful and glorious reign of our Divine Redeemer may be known and enjoyed throughout the whole family of mankind." [23] This prayer request was often repeated by Adams, as, for example, in his 1797 proclamation, in which he asked that the people pray for "speedily bringing on that holy and happy

Commonwealth of *Maffachufetts*.

By the GOVERNOR.

A Proclamation

For a Day of PUBLIC FASTING, HUMILIATION and PRAYER.

THE fupreme Ruler of the Univerfe, having been pleafed, in the courfe of his Providence, to eftablifh the Independence of the United States of AMERICA, and to caufe them to affume their rank, among the nations of the Earth, and blefs them with Liberty, Peace and Plenty ; we ought to be led by *Religious* feelings of Gratitude ; and to walk before Him, in all Humility, according to his moft Holy Law.—But, as the depravity of our Hearts has, in fo many inftances drawn us afide from the path of duty, fo that we have frequently offended our Divine and Merciful Benefactor ; it is therefore highly incumbent on us, according to the ancient and laudable practice of our pious Anceftors, to open the year by a public and folemn FAST.—That with true repentance and contrition of Heart, we may unitedly implore the forgivenefs of our Sins, through the merits of JESUS CHRIST, and humbly fupplicate our Heavenly FATHER, to grant us the aids of his Grace, for the amendment of our Hearts and Lives, and vouchfafe his fmiles upon our

SAMUEL ADAM'S 1795 PROCLAMATION

period when the kingdom of our Lord and Savior Jesus Christ may be everywhere established, and all the people willingly bow to the sceptre of Him who is the Prince of Peace." [24]

Samuel Adams was a strong and outspoken Christian – a fact confirmed both in his private writings and in the official public records. He was such an important leader that he, too, has been honored with an individual statute, located in East Central Hall.

Religious proclamations acknowledging God and calling on His aid (like those already seen from Jonathan Trumbull, John Hancock, and Samuel Adams) were frequent from our Founders, not only in their individual state leadership roles as governors but also in their collective national leadership

SAMUEL ADAMS

roles in Congress. For example, during the Revolution, Congress issued no less than fifteen national prayer proclamations. [25] Those proclamations, each written by different committees composed of different Founding Fathers, were *all* characterized by strong Biblical language. This should come as no surprise, however; after all, in the Declaration of Independence, our Founders announced to the world that they were proceeding "with a *firm reliance* on Divine Providence"; and the numerous prayer proclamations issued throughout the Revolution prove that they meant what they said.

There are many other Founding Fathers in the Rotunda painting of the signers of the Declaration who are worthy of examination, but it is sufficiently established that numerous Christians were among the signers and that much spiritual depth was represented by the individuals in that one painting.

The Rotunda painting of the surrender of the British at Yorktown depicts the conclusion of the last military battle of the American Revolution. Even though two more years would pass before a final peace treaty was signed, for all practical purposes, after Yorktown, America was free from British laws and policies and was now able to establish her own.

Recall that under British law, it had been illegal to print a Bible in the English language in America. Following Yorktown, America was no longer under that restriction, and a plan was advanced in Congress to print America's very own, very first, English-language Bible.

This plan was presented by publisher Robert Aitken of Philadelphia, who offered his own presses for the project. Interestingly, according to the congressional documents accompanying this proposal, on January 21, 1781, the Bible was described to Congress as "a neat edition of the Holy Scriptures for the use of schools." [26]

ROBERT AITKEN

Congress approved the plan and appointed a committee to oversee the printing of the Bible. The result was what has now become one of the rarest books in America – indeed, in the world: the first Bible printed in the English language in America. The front of that Bible contains the endorsement that "The United States in Congress assembled . . . recommend this edition of the Bible to the inhabitants of the United States." This Bible was the result of our Founding Fathers and the American Congress!

THE "BIBLE OF THE REVOLUTION"

Whereupon,
RESOLVED,
THAT the United States in Congress assembled highly approve the pious and laudable undertaking of Mr. Aitken, as subservient to the interest of religion, as well as an instance of the progress of arts in this country, and being satisfied from the above report of his care and accuracy in the execution of the work, they recommend this edition of the Bible to the inhabitants of the United States, and hereby authorise him to publish this Recommendation in the manner he shall think proper.

CHA. THOMSON, Sec'ry.

THE CONGRESSIONAL ENDORSEMENT OF THE BIBLE

The surrender at Yorktown occurred in 1781, the "Bible of the Revolution" was printed in 1782, and the peace treaty with Great Britain was signed in 1783. Interestingly, even that peace treaty – negotiated and signed by John Adams, Benjamin Franklin, and John Jay – reflects the strong religious sentiments of our Founders. For example, notice its opening declaration: "In the Name of the most Holy and undivided Trinity. Amen!" [27] (A copy of the original treaty can still be seen at the John Quincy Adams State Drawing Room in the U. S. State Department in Washington, D. C.)

SIGNATURES ON THE
1783 TREATY

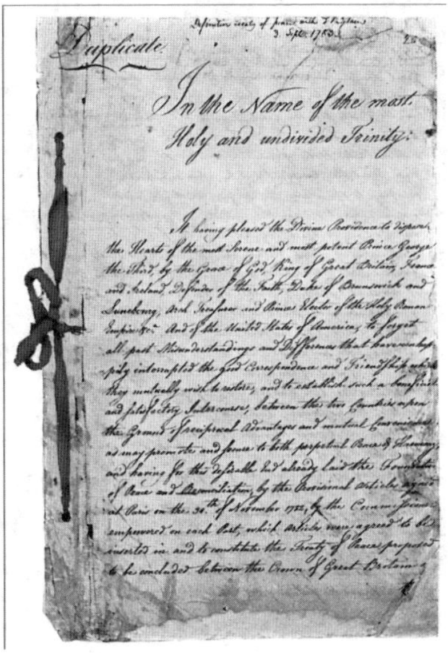

THE 1783 PEACE TREATY

When word of the signed peace treaty reached America, George Washington officially resigned as Commander-in-Chief. In the final of the eight pictures in the Rotunda, George Washington is informing his military staff and the leaders of Congress of his resignation (see page 12). Washington then sent a circular letter to the thirteen governors and State legislatures informing them of his resignation. In that letter, Washington rejoiced in America's recent successes and then closed by offering this prayer for the States and the governors:

I now make it my earnest prayer that God would have you and the State over which you preside in His holy protection, – that He would incline the hearts of the citizens to cultivate a spirit of subordination and obedience to government, – to entertain a brotherly affection and a love for one another, for their fellow citizens of the United States at large, and particularly for their brethren who have served in the field, – and finally, that He would most graciously be pleased to dispose us all to do

THE
LAST OFFICIAL
ADDRESS,
OF HIS EXCELLENCY
General WASHINGTON,
TO THE
Legiflatures of the United States.
TO WHICH IS ANNEXED,
A
COLLECTION OF PAPERS RELATIVE TO
HALF-PAY,
AND COMMUTATION OF
HALF-PAY,
Granted by CONGRESS to the
OFFICERS of the ARMY.
HARTFORD:
PRINTED BY HUDSON AND GOODWIN,
M.DCC.LXXXIII.

WASHINGTON'S RESIGNATION

justice, to love mercy, and to demean ourselves with that charity, humility, and [peaceful] temper of the mind which were the characteristics of the Divine Author of our blessed religion, without an humble imitation of whose example in these things, we can never hope to be a happy nation. [28]

PRESIDENT GARFIELD

The final thing George Washington reminds the governors and States is that if they don't imitate Jesus, America won't be a happy nation.

One of the statues in the Rotunda is of our 20th President, James A. Garfield. Garfield, according to his own account, experienced a miraculous intervention of God in his life which saved him from certain drowning in the Ohio-Pennsylvania canal. His is a wonderful story, told in his biography, *From Log-Cabin to the White House*. [29] Following the Providential intervention that literally saved his life, Garfield gave his heart to the Lord, committed his life to Christ, and became a minister of the Gospel.

GARFIELD LETTER
DESCRIBING REVIVAL

In fact, in one of his letters, he describes a revival in which he personally preached the Gospel 19 times, with 34 individuals coming to Christ and 31 of them being baptized. [30] Although such activities are not typically associated with our Presidents today, this was part of the life of James A. Garfield, the 20th President of the United States and a minister of the Gospel of Jesus Christ!

SMALL HOUSE ROTUNDA

The Small House Rotunda connects the main Rotunda with the Old House Chamber. In the Small House Rotunda there are three statues, including one of the Reverend John Peter Gabriel Muhlenberg.

REV. JOHN PETER MUHLENBERG

In the 1770s, Reverend Muhlenberg pastored two churches in the tiny town of Woodstock, Virginia, on the west side of the Blue Ridge mountains. One of those churches was an English-speaking Episcopal church; the other was a German-speaking Lutheran church. In addition to pastoring those two churches, Reverend Muhlenberg was also a member of the Virginia legislature.

By January 1776, even though it would still be months before the Declaration was signed, armed conflict was fully underway in America. In fact, British troops were already at work in Virginia; they had marched on Williamsburg and seized the patriots' gunpowder and munitions. Patrick Henry rallied 5,000 Virginians to retake those munitions or demand full payment from the British for what had been seized.

In mid-January, Pastor Muhlenberg returned from the State legislature in Williamsburg to his churches in Woodstock, and on January 21, 1776, he stood in his pulpit and delivered what was to become his Farewell Sermon. He preached that day from the passage in Ecclesiastes 3, that to everything there is a time and a season – a time to be born, a time to die, etc. When he arrived at verse 8 (that there is a time for peace and a time for war), he confirmed to his congregation that this indeed was not a time of peace but was instead a time of war – that Virginia had already been forced into the conflict. He then bowed his head and offered a dismissal prayer.

However, instead of following his usual custom after his sermon of going off to the vestry room to disrobe after his sermon, on this occasion he began to disrobe in front of the congregation. When he finally shed his clerical robes, he stood before them in the full uniform of a military officer!

He marched to the back of the church, reminding his parishioners that if they did not get involved and protect their liberties, they would have no liberties left to protect. Outside the church, Pastor Muhlenberg then ordered drummers to beat for recruits, and some 300 men from his congregations joined him that day. They became known as the Eighth Virginia Regiment.

This gallant cleric went on to become one of America's highest ranking military officers. He finished the American Revolution with the rank of Major-General (one of only 17 officers in the Continental Army to achieve that rank), and he is portrayed in the Rotunda picture of the surrender of the British at Yorktown.

Pastor Muhlenberg's statue in the Small House Rotunda depicts the moment in which he removed his clerical robes to reveal his military uniform to the congregation – yet another example of America's rich spiritual heritage depicted so widely throughout the Capitol building.

Not surprisingly, John Peter Gabriel Muhlenberg had a brother who was also a minister and who is also featured in a prominent location in the Capitol. His brother was the Reverend Frederick

Augustus Muhlenberg, pastor of a church in New York City.

Frederick had at first been critical of his brother's becoming involved, as a minister, in the defense of liberty. [31] But when the British arrived in New York City in 1777, they drove Frederick from his own church and then desecrated the building. Frederick thus found himself rethinking his position, and, like his brother, he, too, made the decision to get involved.

REV. FREDERICK AUGUSTUS MUHLENBERG,
SPEAKER OF THE HOUSE

You can find a large portrait of Frederick Augustus Muhlenberg hanging in the Capitol directly behind the current House Chamber in what is called the Speaker's Lobby – a room filled with portraits of all the previous Speakers of the House (and a room closed to the general public). Why is a portrait of the Reverend Frederick Augustus Muhlenberg prominently displayed there? Because in 1789, he became America's very first Speaker of the U. S. House of Representatives. In fact, his signature is one of only two on the Bill of Rights. Another remarkable contribution to American liberty by yet another minister of the Gospel!

SIGNATURE OF REV. MUHLENBERG ON THE BILL OF RIGHTS

OLD HOUSE CHAMBER
(NATIONAL STATUARY HALL)

Beyond the Small House Rotunda is the Old Chamber of the House of Representatives, now called National Statuary Hall. When the House moved into the Capitol in November of 1800, this room did not yet exist. The House then met downstairs on the opposite side of the Rotunda in what is now the Senate side – the first part of the Capitol building to be completed. (Originally the House, Senate, and Supreme Court all met in that one wing.)

In 1807, a second part of the Capitol – the House wing – was completed, and the House moved across the Capitol into its new chamber (now Statuary Hall). Those original Senate and House buildings were separate and were connected only by a wooden walkway (see page 6 for a picture) until permanently joined together by the Rotunda in 1824.

THE OLD HOUSE CHAMBERS
(NOW CALLED NATIONAL STATUARY HALL)

The House, after moving into its new building in 1807, remained here – in the Old House Chamber – until 1857 when it moved into the chamber it currently occupies. (In the current House Chamber, prominently displayed above the Speaker's rostrum is the declaration, "In God We Trust." Around the top of the Chamber walls are images of 23 great lawgivers from across the centuries, including Blackstone, Grotius, and Hammurabi. In the middle, at the back, is Moses, looking down on the proceedings of the House. Significantly, Moses – the lawgiver of the Bible – is the only one of the lawgivers honored with a full face view; all others have only a side profile.)

SOME OF THE 23 LAWGIVERS PICTURED IN THE HOUSE CHAMBERS. L TO R: BLACKSTONE (ENGLISH), GROTIUS (DUTCH), HAMMURABI (BABYLONIAN), MOSES (JEWISH, OF THE BIBLE)

Many famous statesmen conducted their deliberations for the nation in the Old House Chamber. In fact, there are eight bronze plaques embedded in the Chamber floor showing the location of the desks of House members who were also Presidents. These eight include James Buchanan, Millard Fillmore, Abraham Lincoln, Andrew Johnson, Franklin Pierce, James K. Polk, John Tyler, and the venerable John Quincy Adams.

You may recall something of the remarkable story of John Quincy Adams. He grew up during the American Revolution, and by the age of eight, he could perform musket drills with precision – and had proven so at the command of the famous Massachusetts Minutemen who visited his father's house. [32] Although John Quincy Adams was too young to soldier, he did end up serving overseas during the Revolution. At the amazingly young age of 11, he was assigned the task of being secretary to his father, John Adams, America's Ambassador to the British Court

of Saint James. And at the still tender age of 14, he was appointed to be the official diplomatic secretary to Francis Dana, America's Ambassador to Russia.

After the Revolution, John Quincy Adams was appointed as an American Ambassador by President George Washington, who called Adams "the most valuable public character we have abroad." [33] John Quincy continued to hold foreign assignments until the Presidency of Thomas Jefferson, at which time he was elected

JOHN QUINCY ADAMS

to the U. S. Senate. Under President Madison, John Quincy Adams returned to foreign diplomacy; under President Monroe he became Secretary of State; and following Monroe, he became President.

After finishing his Presidency, John Quincy Adams, then 62 years of age, was elected to serve as a member of the House of Representatives, becoming the only President ever to serve in Congress *after* his Presidency. This distinguishes John Quincy Adams from the other

JOHN QUINCY ADAMS
6TH PRESIDENT

JOHN TYLER
10TH PRESIDENT

JAMES K. POLK
11TH PRESIDENT

MILLARD FILLMORE
13TH PRESIDENT

FRANKLIN PIERCE
14TH PRESIDENT

JAMES BUCHANAN
15TH PRESIDENT

ABRAHAM LINCOLN
16TH PRESIDENT

ANDREW JOHNSON
17TH PRESIDENT

EIGHT PRESIDENTS SERVED AS CONGRESSMEN IN THE OLD HOUSE CHAMBER

seven Presidents honored in the Old House Chamber; they went from the House to the Presidency, whereas John Quincy Adams went from the Presidency to the House. John Quincy Adams served in the Old House Chamber until he met death in that room in the midst of his congressional duties in 1848.

Several speeches that this President delivered while a member of the House come closer to sermons than speeches. One such was a Fourth of July oration delivered in 1837 as he was approaching his 69th birthday.

At that Independence Day celebration, John Quincy Adams began his speech by asking two questions. First he queried: "Why is it, friends and fellow citizens, that you are here assembled? Why is it, that, entering upon the sixty-second year of our national existence, you have honored [me] with an invitation to address you?" [34] The answer was quite simple: it was because he was old enough to remember what had happened – he had been an eye-witness and could relate the actual story to them.

JQA'S 1837 ORATION

Mr. Adams next asked, "Why is it that next to the birthday of the Savior of the world, your most joyous and most venerated festival [occurs] on this day?" [35] That is, why were Christmas and the Fourth of July our two most-celebrated holidays in America? He answered his own question with these words:

> Is it not that in the chain of human events the birthday of the nation is indissolubly linked with the birthday of the Savior? That it forms a leading event in the progress of the Gospel dispensation? Is it not that the Declaration of Independence first organized the social compact on the foundation of the Redeemer's mission on Earth? – That it laid the cornerstone of human government on the first precepts of Christianity? [36]

For well over an hour he continued his speech, confirming that Christianity was not only the basis of, but the reason for, our national independence.

John Quincy Adams was an outspoken Christian and an avid student of the Bible. He made it his practice to read through the Bible – in its entirety – once every year. [37] It is not surprising, then, that John Quincy wanted his children to grow up knowing the Bible and how to study it.

The difficulty with his desire was that during the time that his son, George Washington Adams, was growing up, John Quincy Adams was overseas serving as a diplomat. Therefore, in order to teach his son how to study the Bible, between 1811 and 1813 he wrote nine lengthy letters instructing his son how to get the most from a study of God's Word.

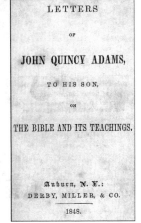

Thirty years after he had written these letters, others found out about them and believed they would be beneficial for all young people. So, those letters were published in a small book: *Letters of John Quincy Adams to His Son, on the Bible and its Teachings.* Today, we rarely think of a President as the author of a book on how to study the Bible, but John Quincy Adams was.

The circumstances surrounding the death of John Quincy Adams are of particular interest, for death in those days was viewed differently from what it is today. Since the Bible teaches in Hebrews 2:14-15 that one indication of a genuine relationship with Christ was a freedom from the fear of death, observers were interested in how an individual reacted when he faced death. As one political historian in 1854 noted:

> [I]t is customary, even among Christian people, to withhold final judgment of a man's Christian character till it is seen how he makes his death. The manner of a man's death often works a change – sometimes a revolution – in public opinion respecting the nature of his life. [38]

JQA THE YEAR
BEFORE HIS DEATH

What, then, did observers see when John Quincy Adams faced death? That occasion occurred in the Old House Chamber on Monday, February 21, 1848. A local newspaper reporter recorded what transpired on that day:

> Just after the yeas and nays were taken on a question, and the Speaker had risen to put another question to the House, a sudden cry was heard on the left of the chair, "Mr. Adams is dying!" Turning our eyes to the spot, we beheld the venerable man in the act of falling over the left arm of his chair, while his right arm was extended, grasping his desk for support. He would have dropped upon the floor had he not been caught in the arms of the member sitting next to him. A great sensation was created in the House; members from all quarters rushing from their seats and gathering round the fallen statesman, who was immediately lifted in to the area in front of the Clerk's table. The Speaker instantly suggested that some gentlemen move an adjournment, which being promptly done, the House adjourned. A sofa was brought, and Mr. Adams, in a state of perfect helplessness, though not of entire insensibility, was gently laid upon it. The sofa was then taken up and borne out of the Hall into the Rotunda, where it was set down, and the members of both Houses, and strangers, who were fast crowding around, were with some difficulty repressed, and an open space cleared in its immediate vicinity; but a medical gentleman, a member of the House, (who was prompt, active, and self-possessed throughout the whole painful scene,) advised that he be removed to the door of the Rotunda opening on the east portico, where a fresh wind was blowing. This was done; but the air being chilly

and loaded with vapor, the sofa was, at the suggestion of Mr. Winthrop, once more taken up and removed to the Speaker's apartment, the doors of which were forthwith closed to all but professional gentlemen and particular friends. While lying in this apartment, Mr. Adams partially recovered the use of his speech, and observed in faltering accents, "This is the end of earth;" but quickly added, "I am composed." . . . Soon after being taken to the Speaker's room, Mr. Adams sank into a state of apparent insensibility, gradually growing weaker and weaker, till on Wednesday evening, February 23rd, at a quarter past 7 o'clock, he expired without a struggle. [39]

OLD CHAMBER OF THE HOUSE SPEAKER
(NOW THE LINDY BOGGS READING ROOM)

"This is the end of earth. I am composed." These were the last words of John Quincy Adams, and they were uttered in a room adjoining the Old House Chamber, a room now called the Lindy Boggs (a former member of the House) Reading Room. At the time that Mr. Adams was carried there, however, that room was the chamber of Speaker of the House Robert Winthrop. It was in the Speaker's chamber that Adams died; that room still contains the actual couch on which he died as well as a bust of him on the wall, recording what occurred in that room. (This room is not open to the public but today serves as the women's reading room and lounge where female Members of Congress may come to rest and relax during congressional proceedings.)

COUCH ON WHICH JQA DIED

In the Old Speaker's Chamber, John Quincy Adams faced death, looked it square in the face with a full awareness of its implications, and displayed no fear. This confirmed to observers that he indeed was a Christian, for he had died as he had lived – with a firm reliance upon His Savior.

> I live in the Faith and Hope of the progressive advancement of Christian Liberty, and expect to abide by the same in death.   J. 2. Adams.

ONE OF JQA'S DECLARATIONS OF FAITH IN CHRIST

As already noted, Robert Winthrop was Speaker of the House when John Quincy Adams died, and it was in Winthrop's office that Adams expired. Robert Winthrop's portrait hangs in the Speaker's Lobby along with the portraits of the other Speakers of the House (this room is also closed to the general public).

THE HON. ROBERT WINTHROP

Robert Winthrop was a statesman, an eminent historian, and a strong Christian. For example, notice this excerpt from a speech he delivered on the Bible and American government. He declared:

All societies of men must be governed in some way or other. The less they may have of stringent State Government, the more they must have of individual self-government. The less they rely on public law or physical force, the more they must rely on private moral restraint. Men, in a word, must necessarily be controlled, either by a power within them, or by a power without them; either by the word of God, or by the strong arm of man; either by the Bible, or by the bayonet. It may do for other countries and other governments to talk about the State supporting Religion. Here, under our own free institutions, it is Religion which must support the State. [40]

This is a powerful truth. As Speaker Winthrop observed, citizens will be controlled either by the Bible or by the bayonet – that is, either by internal self-controls applied from the Word of God or by external coercion and the threat of force. Obviously, the Bible no longer has the powerful public presence that it once did, having been removed by the courts from our schools and public life. The result – as Speaker Robert Winthrop predicted – is an attempt to coerce or force good behavior. Consequently, there has been an explosion of laws, with over 100,000 new laws introduced **each session** in our State legislatures and in the federal Congress. The words of Speaker Robert Winthrop should be remembered today: if men are not self-controlled through the teachings of the Bible, then the only alternative for civil government is coercion.

Speaker of the House Robert Winthrop was another of the many strong Christians who guided the deliberations within the Old House Chamber.

Today, the Old House Chamber is better known as National Statuary Hall – titled this because this room now houses the bulk of the statues found at the Capitol. One of those statues is of Ethan Allen, an officer in the American Revolution who became famous for his capture of the British stronghold of Ticonderoga in northern New York in 1775.

Even though the Declaration of Independence was not signed until the year after Allen's exploit, Great Britain was already warring against her American colonies. In 1774, she had laid siege to Boston and erected a naval blockade. The battles of Charleston, Breed's (or Bunker's) Hill, Lexington, and Concord followed soon after – all long before the Declaration of Independence.

ETHAN ALLEN

As the conflicts spread from Massachusetts into Virginia and other areas, Connecticut, fearing for her own safety, secretly contacted Ethan Allen and requested that he capture Fort Ticonderoga. Even though Ticonderoga was still far away from the scene of any military activity at that time, it was hoped that by this action the British would be forced to pull troops away from their offensive actions against the Americans in order to defend their own forts.

Ethan Allen gathered his Vermont Green Mountain Boys, and late on the night of May 10, 1775, they surrounded the unsuspecting British fort and captured the guards. Having secured the perimeter, Ethan Allen told what occurred next:

> One of the sentries made a pass at one of my officers with a charged bayonet, and slightly wounded him: My first thought was to kill him with my sword; but, in an instant, I altered the design and fury of the blow to a slight cut on the side of the head; upon which he dropped his gun, and asked quarter, which I readily granted him, and demanded of him the place where the commanding officer kept; he showed me a pair of stairs in the front of a barrack, on the west part of the garrison, which led up to a second story in said barrack, to which I immediately repaired, and ordered the commander, Captain de la Place, to come forth instantly, or I would sacrifice the whole garrison; at which the Captain came immediately to the door, with his breeches in his hand; when I ordered him to deliver to me the fort instantly; he asked me by what authority I demanded it: I answered him, "In the name of the great Jehovah, and the Continental Congress." . . . [H]e began to speak again; but I interrupted him, and with my drawn sword over his head, again demanded an immediate surrender of the garrison; with which he then complied. [41]

"In the name of the great Jehovah, and the Continental Congress!" It was this phrase, and the capture of Fort Ticonderoga, which earned Ethan Allen a place in Statuary Hall.

"IN THE NAME OF THE GREAT JEHOVAH AND THE CONTINENTAL CONGRESS!"

Another statue in Statuary Hall is that of Lew Wallace of Indiana. His father was the governor of that State, and Lew Wallace himself held several offices in Indiana. He also served as a distinguished military officer during the Civil War and was the youngest man ever to attain the rank of Major-General. He later became governor of New Mexico and then served as a U. S. Diplomat.

GEN. LEW WALLACE

General Lew Wallace is perhaps best known, however, not for his military or political accomplishments but rather for his literary accom-

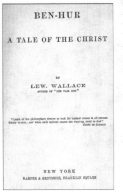

plishments. He was the author of the forever immortalized classic, *Ben-Hur: A Tale of the Christ*, the novel about the life of Judah Ben-Hur. That work, first printed in 1880, swept not only the nation but also the world, being translated into numerous languages.

The impetus for that famous work began in 1876 when General Wallace conversed at length with Robert Ingersoll, a co-officer from the Civil War. Ingersoll, titled by the press as "The Great Agnostic," was the national evangelist for atheism. In his conversation with General Wallace, Ingersoll first forcefully asserted that there was no God, no Devil, and no afterlife, and then challenged Wallace to try to prove that Jesus was the Son of God. [42] Wallace was disturbed by the conversation and found himself ashamed of his own ignorance about the topics raised by Ingersoll, especially his own lack of knowledge about the life of Jesus.

Wallace therefore set out to research the life of Christ, as well as the Jewish and Roman cultures of that day. He studied numerous works, including those by Josephus and Edward Gibbon, and he eventually made a trip to the Holy Land to trace the steps of Christ. As a result of his research, two things happened to General Lew Wallace: one, he became a Christian; and two, he wrote the book that, even today, remains an international classic.

Not only did *Ben-Hur* became the bestselling novel of the nineteenth century, but it probably did more than any other single work to undermine Robert Ingersoll's national message on atheism. *Ben-Hur* inspired Christians as few works before had done; its effect was felt across the nation and all the way to the White House. In fact, former President Ulysses S. Grant, who had not read a novel in ten years, made an exception with *Ben-Hur* and read it through within a day-and-a-half. [43] And President James A. Garfield thought the book so important that he penned a nationally-

PRES. U. S. GRANT   GEN. LEW WALLACE

published letter recommending *Ben-Hur*. [44] President Garfield even asked General Wallace to write more such novels to benefit and strengthen the nation. (President Grant's statue is in the Rotunda, as is the statue of President Garfield.)

General Lew Wallace, commemorated with a statue in Statuary Hall, was one of the most influential Christian authors of the nineteenth century.

Another statue in Statuary Hall is that of Daniel Webster. Daniel Webster was part of the second generation of American statesmen. He was a young man during the American Revolution and grew up listening to the speeches of Presidents George Washington, John Adams, Thomas Jefferson, and James Madison. Following his own entry into politics, Daniel Webster became a leading national figure. He served almost a decade in the U. S. House, nearly two decades in the U. S. Senate, and was the Secretary of State for three different Presidents.

Daniel Webster gained a reputation as an exceptional orator. Whether arguing a case in the Supreme Court or debating a bill in Congress, his powers of argumentation were persuasive. In fact, so great were his skills that it is reported that attorneys, when learning

DANIEL WEBSTER

they would be opposing Daniel Webster, would sometimes withdraw from a case rather than face Webster's genius. [45] Webster's strong commitment to the principles of law and the Constitution earned him the title "The Defender of the Constitution."

As a famous orator, Webster believed that to become a great orator one must study the Word of God. In fact, he regularly practiced his own oratory by reciting the Bible aloud.

There are wonderful anecdotal accounts of visitors gathering just to listen to Daniel Webster read the Bible. [46] They seemed to enjoy especially his readings from the book of Job, for Webster would read that book as if he actually were Job – or one of Job's friends. And when Webster read chapter 38 (when God entered the debate), Webster's voice would thunder and boom, and it seemed as if the doors would rattle off their hinges as he recited the words spoken by the Almighty! Charles Lanman, Webster's personal Senate secretary, recalled:

DANIEL WEBSTER

> We well remember his quotation of some of the verses in the thirty-eighth chapter [of Job]: "Then the Lord answered Job out of the whirlwind, and said, Who is this that darkeneth counsel by words without knowledge? Gird up now thy loins like a man; for I will demand of thee, and answer thou me. Where wast thou when I laid the foundations of the earth? Declare, if thou hast understanding," &c. Mr. Webster was a fine reader, and his recitation of particular passages which he admired was never surpassed and was capable of giving the most exquisite delight to those who could appreciate them. [47]

OLD SENATE CHAMBER

The Old Senate Chamber is where Daniel Webster gave nearly two decades of public service. One of his original artifacts still at the Capitol is his old Senate desk.

That desk is no longer in the Old Senate Chamber because it is still in use today in the current Senate Chamber. (By agreement, the senior Senator from New Hampshire – the State of Webster's birth – is allowed to use the original desk.) However, at the time Webster served in the Senate, he used his desk in the Old Senate Chamber. In the bottom of his desk, Webster took a penknife and inscribed his name,

DANIEL WEBSTER IN THE OLD SENATE CHAMBERS

WEBSTER'S ORIGINAL SENATE DESK

WEBSTER AT HIS SENATE DESK

WEBSTER'S NAME (TOP LEFT)
INSCRIBED INSIDE HIS DESK

and many of those who used his desk after him followed this precedent.

Daniel Webster developed his love for penknives at an early age. In fact, Master James Tappan, one of Daniel's first schoolteachers, told the story of how Daniel received his first penknife:

> Daniel was always the brightest boy in the school. . . . He would learn more in five minutes than any other boy in five hours. . . . One Saturday, I remember, I held up a handsome new jack-knife to the scholars and said the boy who would commit to memory the greatest number of verses in the Bible by Monday morning should have it. Many of the boys did well; but when it came to Daniel's turn to recite, I found that he had committed so much [to memory] that after hearing him repeat some sixty or seventy verses, I was obliged to give up, he telling me [still] that there were several chapters yet that he had learned. Daniel got that jack-knife. [48]

Daniel Webster learned early to love the Bible, and his love for that Book never waned. In fact, on the Fourth of July, 1851, the year before his death, Webster stood just outside the Capitol on its east side and delivered the speech at the laying of the cornerstone for the additions to the Capitol that have now become the current chambers for the House and the Senate. Speaking to the thousands gathered there at the Capitol that day, Webster summed up not only what he had believed throughout his life but also what he believed must continue to be part of America's public policy. He explained:

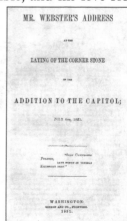

MR. WEBSTER'S ADDRESS

AT THE

LAYING OF THE CORNER STONE

OF THE

ADDITION TO THE CAPITOL;

JULY 4TH, 1851.

WEBSTER'S 1851 SPEECH

Man is not only an intellectual but he is also a religious being, and his religious feelings and habits require cultivation.
Let the religious element in man's nature be neglected – let
him be influenced by no higher motives than low self-inter-
est, and subjected to no stronger restraint than the limits of
civil authority – and he becomes the creature of selfish passion or blind fanaticism. The spectacle of a nation [France],
powerful and enlightened, but without Christian faith, has
been presented . . . as a warning beacon for the nations. On
the other hand, the cultivation of the religious sentiment
represses licentiousness, incites to general benevolence and
the practical acknowledgment of the brotherhood of man,
inspires respect for law and order, and gives strength to the
whole social fabric. [49]

WEBSTER SPOKE TO THE THOUSANDS AT THE CAPITOL ON JULY 4TH, 1851

Daniel Webster did not believe that the public good would ever be served apart from Christianity. As he reminded one public gathering, "Whatever makes men good Christians, makes them good citizens." [50]

Daniel Webster was another of the great leaders here at the Capitol who was outspoken about Christianity both in private and in public and who has received special recognition in the Capitol both with paintings and with a statue in Statuary Hall.

NATIONAL STATUARY HALL

As a final note on National Statuary Hall, in addition to the statues of Ethan Allen, Lew Wallace, and Daniel Webster already discussed, there are numerous other statues commemorating the lives and accomplishments of many famous Christians, including those of missionary and pioneer trailblazer Marcus Whitman with Bible under his arm, missionary Junipero Serra with cross held high, and numerous others.

MARCUS WHITMAN   JUNIPERO SERRA

HOUSE CONNECTING CORRIDOR

In the House Connecting Corridor just beyond Statuary Hall are additional statues, including one of Jonathan Trumbull. However, this is not the John Trumbull who painted the pictures in the Rotunda nor is this the Colonel Jonathan Trumbull whose religious proclamation was presented earlier. Rather, this is the father of them both.

This Jonathan Trumbull was the only governor of the thirteen States to serve in that capacity throughout the entire Revolution. He probably did more than any other single individual to supply men, munitions, and materials to General George Washington. In fact, he became one of Washington's closest friends and confidants; Washington called him "Brother Jonathan"; and whenever he needed counsel or a listening ear, it was to Governor Trumbull he turned.

GOV. JONATHAN TRUMBULL

Jonathan Trumbull had not planned to be a governor, or for that matter, to have a military or political career. Originally, he had studied for the ministry and had served as a preacher of the Gospel. But when his State (Connecticut) asked him to serve as governor, he did not refuse. He held that post for fourteen years, and as soon as the Revolution was over and the peace treaty with Great Britain was signed, he resigned.

The statue pictures him holding his letter of resignation which he sent to the State legislature in October 1783. In that letter, he explains that after fourteen years of leading the state, it is now safe, and he therefore is ready to retire. Why? At age 73, he wanted to return to his ministerial studies! As he told the legislature:

[O]n my advanced stage of life, – a life worn out almost in the constant cares of office, I think it my duty to retire from the busy concerns of public affairs: that at the evening of my days, I may sweeten their decline by devoting myself with less avocation and more attention to the duties of religion, the service of my God, and preparation for a future and happier state of existence, – in which pleasing employment I shall not cease to remember my country, and to make it my ardent prayer that Heaven will not fail to bless her with its choicest favors. [51]

Governor Jonathan Trumbull is another of our many American patriots and heroes who is honored with a statue here at the Capitol, and who was also a minister of the Gospel.

STEPS TO THE HOUSE VISITOR'S GALLERY

Over the landing of the second-floor steps leading up to the Visitors' Gallery for the House of Representatives is a huge painting (20' by 30') of the signing of the Constitution on September 17, 1787.

A GUIDE TO IDENTIFYING SIGNERS OF THE CONSTITUTION

1. GEORGE WASHINGTON, VA
2. BENJAMIN FRANKLIN, PA
3. JAMES MADISON, VA
4. ALEXANDER HAMILTON, NY
5. GOUVERNEUR MORRIS, PA
6. ROBERT MORRIS, PA
7. JAMES WILSON, PA
8. CHARLES COTESWORTH PINCKNEY, SC
9. CHARLES PINCKNEY, SC
10. JOHN RUTLEDGE, SC
11. PIERCE BUTLER, SC
12. ROGER SHERMAN, CT
13. WILLIAM SAMUEL JOHNSON, CT

14. JAMES MCHENRY, MD
15. GEORGE READ, DE
16. RICHARD BASSETT, DE
17. RICHARD DOBBS SPAIGHT, NC
18. WILLIAM BLOUT, NC
19. HUGH WILLIAMSON, NC
20. DANIEL GENIFER OF ST. THOMAS, MD
21. RUFUS KING, MA
22. NATHANIEL GORHAM, MA
23. JONATHAN DAYTON, NJ
24. DANIEL CARROLL, MD
25. WILLIAM FEW, GA
26. ABRAHAM BALDWIN, GA

27. JOHN LANGDON, NH
28. NICHOLAS GILMAN, NH
29. WILLIAM LIVINGSTON, NJ
30. WILLIAM PATERSON, NJ
31. THOMAS MIFFLIN, PA
32. GEORGE CLYMER, PA
33. THOMAS FITZSIMMONS, PA
34. JARED INGERSOLL, PA
35. GUNNING BEDFORD, JR. DE
36. DAVID BREARLEY, NJ
37. JOHN DICKINSON, DE
38. JOHN BLAIR, VA
39. JACOB BROOM, DE
40. WILLIAM JACKSON, SC, SECRETARY

Fifty-five Founding Fathers served at the Convention which produced the Constitution, and thirty-nine of them eventually signed that document. And, as in the painting of the signers of the Declaration, many of their faces and names are unfamiliar today. Let's rediscover something about some of those in the picture.

Begin with Abraham Baldwin. Not only was he the chief founder of the University of Georgia, but in his time he was one of America's youngest theologians. At the age of twenty-one, he was offered a Professorship of Divinity at Yale University, and throughout the American Revolution he served as a military chaplain. Constitution signer Abraham Baldwin was not only a Christian but also a minister of the Gospel.

The man seated at the table is Roger Sherman. He holds a unique position among the Founding Fathers in that he is the only Founder to sign all four of America's founding documents: the Articles of Association in 1774, the Declaration of Independence in 1776, the Articles of Confederation in 1778, and the U. S. Constitution in 1787.

During the Constitutional Convention, Roger Sherman was instrumental in resolving the conflict over representation between the big States and the small States. Sherman's solution, now enshrined in the Constitution, was that Congress should be made up of two bodies: a Senate wherein each State, whether large or small, would have equal strength and an equal vote (favorable to the small States); and a House, wherein each State's strength would be determined by its population (favorable to the big States). After the Constitution was ratified, Sherman became a member of the first Congress where he helped frame the Bill of Rights.

In addition to being a leading statesman, Roger Sherman was also a theologian. In fact, a creed he personally wrote was adopted by his church. Notice his doctrinal position:

ROGER SHERMAN

I believe that there is one only living and true God, existing in three persons, the Father, the Son, and the Holy Ghost, the same in substance, equal in power and glory. That the Scriptures of the Old and New Testaments are a revelation from God, and a complete rule to direct us how we may glorify and enjoy Him. . . . That He made man at first perfectly holy; that the first man sinned, and as he was the public head of his posterity, they all became sinners in consequence of his first transgression, are wholly indisposed to that which is good and inclined to evil, and on account of sin are liable to all the miseries of this life, to death, and to the pains of hell forever. I believe that God . . . did send His own Son to become man, die in the room and stead of sinners, and thus to lay a foundation for the offer of pardon and salvation to all mankind, so as all may be saved who are willing to accept the Gospel offer. . . . I believe a visible church to be a congregation of those who make a credible profession of their faith in Christ, and obedience to Him, joined by the bond of the covenant. . . . I believe that the sacraments of the New Testament are baptism and the Lord's supper. . . . I believe that the souls of believers are at their death made perfectly holy, and immediately taken to glory: that at the end of this world there will be a resurrection of the dead, and a final judgment of all mankind, when the righteous shall be publicly acquitted by Christ the Judge and admitted to everlasting life and glory, and the wicked be sentenced to everlasting punishment. [52]

Roger Sherman, a distinguished Founding Father and a signer of the Constitution, was also a Christian theologian! His contributions to America were so great that he is one of those honored with a statue at the Capitol, located in East Central Hall.

William Samuel Johnson is also seated at the table in the painting. In addition to signing the Constitution, he was also a leading educator of his day, becoming the first president of Columbia (formerly King's) College. In an exercise which we still practice today, Johnson was a speaker at a public graduation. Notice his words to the graduates:

You this day. . . . have, by the favor of Providence and the attention of friends, received a public education, the purpose whereof hath been to qualify you the better to serve your Creator and your country. You have this day invited this audience to witness the progress you have made. . . . Thus you assume the character of scholars, of men, and of citizens. . . . Go, then, . . . and exercise them with diligence, fidelity, and zeal. . . . Your first great duties, you are sensible, are those you owe to Heaven, to your Creator and Redeemer. Let these be ever present to your minds, and exemplified in your lives and conduct. Imprint deep upon your minds the principles of piety towards God, and a reverence and fear of His holy name. The fear of God is the beginning of wisdom and its [practice] is everlasting [happiness]. . . . Reflect deeply and often upon [your] relations [with God]. Remember that it is in God you live and move and have your being, – that, in the language of David, He is about your bed and about your path and spieth out all your ways, – that there is not a thought in your hearts, nor a word upon your tongues, but lo! He knoweth them altogether, and that He will one day call you to a strict account for all your conduct in this mortal life. Remember, too, that you are the redeemed of the Lord, that you are bought with a price, even the inestimable price of the precious blood of the Son of God. Adore Jehovah, therefore, as your God and your Judge. Love, fear, and serve Him as your Creator, Redeemer, and Sanctifier. Acquaint yourselves with Him in His word and holy ordinances. . . . [G]o forth into the world firmly resolved neither to be allured by its vanities nor contaminated by its vices, but to run with patience and perseverance, with firmness and [cheerfulness], the glorious career of religion, honor, and virtue. . . . Finally, . . . in the elegant and expressive language of St. Paul, "Whatsoever things are true, whatsoever things are honest, whatsoever things are just, whatsoever things are pure, whatsoever things are lovely, whatsoever things are of good report, if there be any virtue, and if there be any praise, think on these things" – and do them, and the God of peace shall be with you, to whose most gracious protection I now commend you, humbly imploring Almighty Goodness that He will be your guardian and your guide, your protector and the rock of your defence, your Savior and your God. [53]

This Founding Father and signer of the Constitution delivered sermons from the Bible at public school graduations!

On the far right of the picture is Jacob Broom. Surprisingly, all that can be seen of him in the picture is the top of his head. The reason for this is that he is one of the few Founding Fathers who never had a portrait made. We do know that he was a part of the Constitutional Convention; we do know that he signed the Constitution; but we don't know what he looked like; and the painting therefore omits his face.

One other thing that we do know about Jacob Broom is that he was a devout Christian and raised his children in the Christian faith. One evidence of this is seen in a letter which he wrote to his son, James, in 1794.

James left home to attend college at Princeton, and Jacob, like a good father, was concerned about how his son would behave while away at school. He exhorted his son: "I flatter myself you will be what I wish, but don't be so much flatterer as to relax of your application – don't forget to be a Christian. I have said much to you on this head, and I hope an indelible impression is made." [54]

Jacob Broom – reminding his son to stay true to the Christian teachings in which he was raised! This letter provides more evidence that the

BROOM'S LETTER TO HIS SON

Founding Fathers were indeed men of religious conviction.

Also in the picture over the landing is Alexander Hamilton – honored in several other places throughout the Capitol. He was a signer of the Constitution and, as an author of *The Federalist Papers,* is considered one of the three men most responsible for the ratification of the Constitution.

You may recall that Alexander Hamilton died a premature death (at age 48) at the hands of Aaron Burr in a duel in 1804. For all practical purposes, Hamilton was executed by Burr.

Hamilton and Burr had a long history of political opposition, born chiefly of Hamilton's strong conviction that Burr's character made him completely unfit for public office. Hamilton made this opinion clear to his friends:

> [Burr is] as unprincipled and dangerous a man as any country can boast. . . . [T]here is nothing in his favor. His private

character is not defended by his most partial friends. . . . [He] has no principle, public or private. . . . [H]e is believed by friends as well as foes to be without [honesty or integrity]. . . . [He is] in debt vastly beyond his means of payment, [and] with all [his] habits [of extravagance], he cannot be satisfied with the regular [salary] of any of-

AARON BURR

fice of our government, [and so c]orrupt [methods] will be to him a necessary resource. . . . I could scarcely name a discreet man of either party . . . who does not think Mr. Burr the most unfit man in the United States for . . . office. [55]

As subsequent events later proved, Hamilton's assessment of Burr's character was completely accurate.

Because of his unwavering conviction of Burr's dangerous tendencies, Hamilton did everything he could to keep Burr from gaining any public office. He opposed Burr for State governor, for U. S. President, for foreign diplomat, and for every other position Burr sought. Burr's arrogance did not permit him to suffer such public defeats, and in an attempt to save face, he challenged Hamilton to a duel.

At the time of Burr's challenge to Hamilton, dueling was still an accepted practice in America. If challenged, you could, and usually would, defend your honor in a personal duel. Although as a military leader, Hamilton was trained in the art of war and weaponry, he was part of a slowly growing movement which disapproved of personal duels. He therefore tried to dissuade Burr from the duel, and even offered other recourses – all of which Burr refused.

Hamilton at last conceded to his friends that if he did not face Burr in a duel, he knew that he would be publicly branded as a coward and that his own personal reputation would be so tarnished that he could never again hold public office. He explained:

ALEXANDER HAMILTON

To those who, with me, abhorring the practice of dueling, may think that I ought on no account to have added to the number of bad examples, I answer that my relative situation, as well in public as private, ... impressed on me ... a peculiar necessity not to decline the call. The ability to be in future useful, whether in resisting mischief or [achieving] good . . . would probably be insepa-rable from . . . public prejudice [against me if I refuse]. [56]

Hamilton did not want to fight, yet he knew that he must at least appear to fight – and "appear to fight" is a key phrase. Since it was his personal commitment that he would shoot no man unless it were on a military battlefield in defense of life or country, Hamilton therefore decided not to fire at Aaron Burr but rather to fire his pistol into the air – or even not fire it at all. In those final days before the duel, Hamilton recorded his decision for posterity:

> I have resolved, if ... it pleases God to give me the opportunity, to reserve and throw away my first [shot]; and I have thoughts even of reserving my second [shot] – and thus giving a double opportunity to Col. Burr. [57]

Hamilton believed that Burr would take full advantage of this op-portunity and that Burr would likely shoot him down.

Believing that he would probably die as a result of his decision not to fire at Burr, Hamilton spent the final days before the duel prepar-ing himself and his affairs, both temporal and spiritual, for his own death. On the temporal side, he wrote out his last will and testament, making preparations for the support of his wife and children. On the spiritual side, he spent those last few days preparing anew for eternity, making completely sure that there was absolutely nothing standing between him and his Savior.

(Over a decade earlier, Hamilton had become involved in an adulterous affair for which he had completely repented, sought forgiveness, and properly amended his life. Nevertheless, despite that earlier recommitment to his faith and its principles, he still desired to have nothing stand between him and his God.)

THE HAMILTON-BURR DUEL

The duel – on the morning of July 11, 1804 – went exactly as Hamilton had anticipated: Hamilton did not fire at Burr, but Burr nevertheless shot Hamilton. Hamilton, mortally wounded, was carried to his house where he lingered for another day before he died.

In those final twenty four hours while life still remained in him, Hamilton called for two ministers, the Rev. J. M. Mason and the Rev. Benjamin Moore, to pray with him and administer Communion to him. Each of those two ministers reported what happened in those final hours. The Rev. Mason recounted:

[General Hamilton said] "I went to the field determined not to take his life." He repeated his disavowal of all intention to hurt Mr. Burr; the anguish of his mind in recollecting what had passed; and his humble hope of forgiveness from his God. I recurred to the topic of the divine compassion; the freedom of pardon in the Redeemer Jesus to perishing sinners. "That grace, my dear General, which brings salvation, is rich, rich" – "Yes," interrupted he, "it is rich grace." "And on that grace," continued I, "a sinner has

REV. MASON'S ACCOUNT

the highest encouragement to repose his confidence, because it is tendered to him upon the surest foundation; the Scripture testifying that we have redemption through the blood of Jesus, the forgiveness of sins according to the richness of His grace." Here the General, letting go my hand, which he had held from the moment I sat down at his bed side, clasped his hands together, and, looking up towards Heaven, said, with emphasis, "I have a tender reliance on the mercy of the Almighty, through the merits of the Lord Jesus Christ." [58]

The Rev. Benjamin Moore reported:

[I]mmediately after he was brought from [the field] . . . a message was sent informing me of the sad event, accompanied by a request from General Hamilton that I would come to him for the purpose of administering the Holy Communion. I went. . . . I proceeded to converse with him on the subject of his receiving the Communion; and told him that with respect to the qualifications of those who wished to become partakers of that holy ordinance, my inquires could not be made in language more expressive than that which was used by our [own] Church. – [I asked], "Do you sincerely repent of your sins past? Have you a lively faith in God's mercy through Christ, with a thankful remembrance of the death of Christ? And are you disposed to live in love and charity with all men?" He lifted up his hands and said, "With the utmost sincerity of heart I can answer those questions in the affirmative – I have no ill will against Col. Burr. I met him with a fixed resolution to do him no harm – I forgive all that happened." . . . The Communion was then administered, which he received with great devotion, and his heart afterwards appeared to be perfectly at rest. I saw him again this morning, when, with his last faltering words, he expressed a strong confidence in the mercy of God through the intercession of the Redeemer. I remained with him until 2 o'clock this afternoon, when death closed the awful scene – he expired without a struggle, and almost without a groan. By reflecting on this melancholy event, let the humble believer be encouraged ever to hold fast that precious faith which is the only source of true consolation in the last extremity of nature. [And l]et the infidel be persuaded to abandon his opposition to that Gospel which the strong, inquisitive, and comprehensive mind of a Hamilton embraced. [59]

One other consequence of Hamilton's untimely death was that it permanently halted the forma- tion of a religious society Hamilton had proposed. What was that society? Hamilton suggested that it be named the Christian Constitutional Society, and listed two goals for its formation: first, the support of the Christian religion; and second, the support of the Constitution of the United States. This or- ganization was to have numerous clubs throughout each state which would meet regularly and work to elect to office those who reflected the goals of the Christian Constitutional Society. [60]

This proposed society to support the Christian religion was the design of Alexander Hamilton, another of the many men of faith who had a sig-

ALEXANDER HAMILTON

nificant influence on the founding of American government and who has been honored with a statue in the Rotunda.

PINCKNEY (LEFT) AND LANGDON (RIGHT)

Charles Cotesworth Pinckney and John Langdon are two oth- ers in the picture of the signing of the Constitution. There is a strong connection between these two signers and the 1997 landmark Promise Keepers Rally which took place on the National Mall front- ing the Capitol on the west. The Promise Keepers Rally – a gathering of between one and two million men dedicated to being Godly influences in their family and their world – has been described by official observers as the largest gathering ever to occur at the Capitol.

The American Bible Society prepared one million copies of a special commemorative edition of the Bible for that rally, and those million Bibles went quickly. Of course, it is not unusual for the American Bible Society to distribute a million Bibles in one day, for they distribute upwards of 200 million Bibles in a single year. The Society which handed out those million Bibles at the Promise Keepers Rally was founded two centuries ago with the help of signers of the Constitution, Charles Cotesworth Pinckney and John Langdon.

The original constitution of the American Bible Society lists its founders, and the list is quite impressive. Its first president was the Honorable Elias Boudinot, who had served as a president of the Continental Congress, signed the final peace treaty with Great Britain to end the Revolution, and helped frame the Bill of Rights. Incidentally, Elias Boudinot also authored a book called *The Age of Revelation* – a Biblical refutation of Thomas Paine's anti-religious work, *The Age of Reason*.

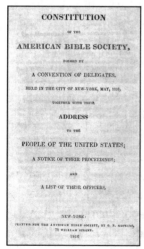

ORIGINAL ABS CONSTITUTION

ELIAS BOUDINOT, FIRST PRESIDENT OF THE ABS

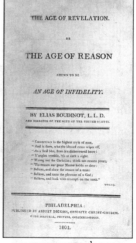

ELIAS BOUDINOT'S BOOK

The original vice-presidents of the American Bible Society, in addition to John Langdon and Charles Cotesworth Pinckney, also included several members of the Supreme Court: Justice John Jay, the original Chief Justice of the Supreme Court and one of the three authors of *The Federalist Papers;* Justice Bushrod Washington; and Justice Smith Thompson, a former Secretary of the Navy. (Justice John Marshall – an officer on George Washington's staff during the Revolution, a Secretary of State under President John Adams, and the fourth Chief Justice of the Supreme Court – later became a vice-president of the American Bible Society.)

Other founding officers of the American Bible Society included Felix Grundy, Attorney General under President Martin Van Buren; William Wirt, Attorney General under Presidents James Monroe and John Quincy Adams; Matthew Clarkson, Major-General during the American Revolution; Caleb Strong, a delegate to the Constitutional Convention and a governor of Massachusetts; William Gray, Lieutenant Governor of Massachusetts; John Cotton Smith, Governor of Connecticut; Jonas Galusha, Governor of Vermont; William Jones, Governor of Rhode Island; Isaac Shelby, Governor of Kentucky; George Madison, a later governor of Kentucky; Thomas Worthington, Governor of Ohio; Thomas Posey, Governor of Indiana; James Brown, U. S. Senator from Louisiana; William Tilghman, Chief Justice of the Supreme Court of Pennsylvania; William Gaston, Justice of the Supreme Court of North Carolina; and Richard Varick, Attorney General and Speaker of the House in New York. In fact, the original founders of the American Bible Society were a veritable "Who's Who" of American political founders. [61]

Another of the signers who appears in the painting of the signing of the Constitution is James McHenry. James McHenry was a military officer who served during the American Revolution as an aide to General George Washington. When Washington became President, he selected McHenry as Secretary

JOHN LANGDON
CONSTITUTION SIGNER

C. C. PINCKNEY
CONSTITUTION SIGNER

ELIAS BOUDINOT
PRESIDENT OF CONGRESS

JOHN JAY
U. S. SUPREME COURT

BUSHROD WASHINGTON
U. S. SUPREME COURT

SMITH THOMPSON
U. S. SUPREME COURT

WILLIAM WIRT
U. S. ATTORNEY GENERAL

FELIX GRUNDY
U. S. ATTORNEY GENERAL

CALEB STRONG
GOVERNOR OF MASS.

RICHARD VARICK
NEW YORK ATTORNEY GENERAL

WILLIAM GASTON
N. C. SUPREME COURT

ISAAC SHELBY
GOVERNOR OF KENTUCKY

SOME OF THE ORIGINAL FOUNDERS OF THE AMERICAN BIBLE SOCIETY

of War, and McHenry continued in that post under President John Adams. (The fort named for this signer of the Constitution – Fort McHenry – was the site under bombardment observed by Francis Scott Key when he wrote the "Star Spangled Banner.")

James McHenry founded the Baltimore Bible Society, which has since changed its name to the Maryland Bible Society. [62] Notice James McHenry's forceful declaration on the importance of the Bible in American society:

> [P]ublic utility pleads most forcibly for the general distribution of the Holy Scriptures. The doctrine they preach – the obligations they impose – the punishment they threaten – the rewards they promise – the stamp and image of divinity they bear which produces a conviction of their truths – [these] can alone secure to society, order and peace, and to our courts of justice and constitutions of government, purity, stability, and usefulness. In vain, without the Bible, we increase penal laws and draw entrenchments around our institutions. Bibles are strong entrenchments. Where they abound, men cannot pursue wicked courses. [63]

Constitution signer James McHenry believed that the Bible was the best preventive against crime and the best safeguard of civil government.

Numerous others who signed the Constitution were also strong Christians and are highlighted in other parts of the Capitol. However, before moving downstairs to the original Senate Chamber (now called the Old Supreme Court Chamber), allow one other Founder in the picture of the signing of the Constitution – George Washington – to be the focal point illustrating how revisionism works to create the myth that our Founding Fathers were not Christians.

George Washington's accomplishments are well known: Commander-in-Chief of the

Continental Army during the American Revolution, President of the Convention which produced the Constitution, first President of the United States, and the President who oversaw the creation of the Bill of Rights. Having given fifty years of his life to such prominent leadership roles, he is justifiably called "The Father of His Country."

George Washington was also a prolific writer. In fact, there are nearly one hundred volumes of his published writings, not including the countless volumes written about him by his friends and contemporaries. In 1855, John Frederick Schroeder went through the available writings and divided Washington's pithy statements into a variety of topical categories. Schroeder compiled those sayings into a book, *The Maxims of Washington*, dividing Washington's maxims into four categories: political, social, moral, and religious. [64]

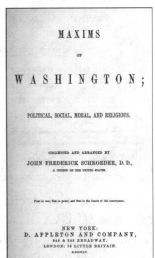

In that book, Schroeder introduced each category of maxims with testimonials about Washington from his contemporaries. These testimonials came from noted individuals, many of whom are honored here at the Capitol, including Ben Franklin, General Marquis de Lafayette, John Paul Jones, John Hancock, Alexander Hamilton, and numerous others.

In the section on Washington's religious maxims, those who testified included J. M. Sewell, a poet and songwriter friend of Washington who declared that Washington "was a firm believer in the Christian religion"; [65] Chief Justice John Marshall, who served on Washington's staff during the Revolution and who declared, "He was a sincere believer in the Christian faith"; [66] Elias Boudinot, who served as a President of Congress during the Revolution and as a member of Congress under President Washington, and who declared "The General was a Christian"; [67] J. Smith, a soldier in the Revolution and a U. S. Congressman throughout Washington's

IV. CHRISTIANITY.

1. *AUTHOR AND SPIRIT OF THE GOSPEL.*

He was a firm believer in the Christian religion; and at his first entrance on his civil administration, he made it known, and adhered to his purpose, that no secular business could be transacted with him, on the day set apart by Christians for the worship of the Deity.   J. M. SEWALL, *Portsmouth, N. H.*, 1799.

To Christian institutions he gave the countenance of his example.
                                                    Rev. J. T. KIRKLAND.

He was a sincere believer in the Christian faith.   *Chief Justice* MARSHALL.

The General was a Christian.   *Judge* BOUDINOT.

He had all the genuine mildness of Christianity, with all its force. He was neither ostentatious nor ashamed of his Christian profession.
                                         J. SMITH, *Exeter, N. H., Feb.* 22, 1800.

He was a professor of Christianity.
                           Rev. DEVEREUX JARRATT, *Dinwiddie Co., Va.*, 1800.
A Christian, in faith and practice.   JARED SPARKS.

QUOTES ABOUT GEORGE WASHINGTON FROM THE ORIGINAL 1855 *MAXIMS OF WASHINGTON*

Presidency, who declared that George Washington was "no[t] ashamed of his Christian profession"; [68] and the Reverend Devereux Jarratt, a Virginia minister who declared that Washington "was a professor of Christianity." [69] There are several additional testimonials scattered throughout the chapter, but there is no doubt that those who knew George Washington personally declared unequivocally that he was a Christian.

The original *Maxims of Washington* was recently reprinted in its entirety [70] – at least, *almost* in its entirety. The difference was that the introduction to each section was changed; and in the section on Washington's religious maxims, the personal, eye-witness testimonies from those who declared George Washington to be a Christian were replaced by the commentary of a present-day professor claiming that George Washington was a deist, not a Christian. [71] This is revisionism – rejecting the testimony of eyewitnesses and replacing it with the opinion of a so-called "expert" two hundred years after the fact.

A further example of how revisionism attempts to misportray the religious faith of George Washington recently appeared in an ad in a national magazine. [72] That ad (promoting a new book) claimed "George Washington was Unitarian" and not Christian. The only problem with the charge is that it is not true. All of George Washington's religious ties were to the Episcopal church, which did not hold Unitarian beliefs; furthermore, Washington died in 1799, and the Unitarians did not even organize until 1818 – nineteen years *after* Washington's death!

Also in stark contrast to the current revisionist changes stands perhaps the most concise testimony of George Washington's faith – that of Nelly Custis, Washington's adopted daughter. Nelly lived with the Washingtons at Mount Vernon for twenty years, from her childhood until her own marriage. In a letter she wrote to Jared Sparks, a chaplain of Congress, Nelly confirmed Washington's Christianity:

[George Washington] attended church [in Virginia] at Alexandria when the weather and roads permitted a ride of ten miles [– a two or thee hour journey, one way]. [While serving as President i]n New York and Philadelphia he never omitted attendance at

NELLY (RIGHT) GREW UP AT MT. VERNON

church in the morning, unless detained by [sickness]. [Sunday] afternoon was spent in his own room at home.... [and] visiting and visitors were prohibited [on Sundays]. No one in church attended to the services with more reverential respect. . . . I should have thought it the greatest heresy to doubt his firm belief in Christianity. His life, his writings, prove that he was a Christian. . . . [And w]hen my aunt . . . died suddenly at Mount Vernon, before they [understood that she was dead], [General Washington] knelt by her and prayed most fervently, most affectingly, for her recovery. . . . [Martha] and [George] were . . . perfectly united and happy. . . . [and Martha] had no doubts, no fears for him. After forty years of devoted affection and uninterrupted happiness [in their marriage], she resigned [George at his death], without a murmur, into the arms of his Savior and his God, with the assured hope of his eternal [happiness in Heaven]. Is it necessary that any one should [prove], "General Washington [claimed to be] a believer in Christianity?" As well may we question his patriotism [and his] devotion to his country! [73]

GEORGE WASHINGTON.

The General Assembly of the Commonwealth of Virginia have caused this Statue to be erected as a monument of affection and gratitude to
GEORGE WASHINGTON;
who, uniting to the endowments of the *Hero* the virtues of the *Patriot*, and exerting both in establishing the Liberties of his Country has rendered his name dear to his Fellow Citizens, and given the world an immortal example of true Glory. Done, in the year of
CHRIST,
One thousand seven hundred and eighty eight, and in the year of the Commonwealth the twelfth.

GEORGE WASHINGTON

Even though his adopted daughter declared that one might as well question the patriotism of George Washington as question his Christianity, nevertheless, through the work of secularists and revisionists who ignore eyewitness accounts and documented writings, George Washington – and other Founding Fathers – has wrongly been labeled "deist." The historical records – including those here at the Capitol – clearly demonstrate otherwise.

CONGRESSIONAL PRAYER CHAPEL

There is a room at the Capitol which honors the true faith of George Washington and which reflects the true George Washington of a pre-revisionist era. That room is the Congressional Prayer Room, located just off the main Rotunda. This room was opened in 1954, the same year in which Congress added the phrase "under God" to the pledge of allegiance. Since the chapel is actively used today by Congressmen who want to pray and seek God, it is not open to the public.

In the front of this Congressional Chapel is an inspiring stained-glass window portraying George Washington kneeling in prayer – a position that, according to Washington's friends and observers, was his frequent prayer posture. [74] Above his picture is the declaration, "This Nation Under God," and surrounding Washington is the Bible verse from Psalm 16:1 declaring, "Preserve me, O God, for in Thee do I put my trust."

STAINED-GLASS WINDOW IN
THE CONGRESSIONAL CHAPEL

SMALL SENATE ROTUNDA

The vestibule (Small Senate Rotunda) fronting the original Senate Chamber on the first floor of the Capitol contains two plaques of interest. The first commemorates an event that happened on May 24, 1844, when Samuel F. B. Morse, the inventor of the telegraph and the father of the Morse code (as well as a distinguished painter), sent the first telegraphic message – a message which came from the Capitol: "What hath God wrought!"

The second plaque in the small Senate Rotunda commemorates an event which occurred in the adjoining room (the original Senate chamber, now called the Old Supreme Court Chamber). This part of the Capitol was the first part to be completed (in 1800 – see the picture on page 6) and at that time, the House, the Senate, and the Supreme Court all met in this one small building.

For a decade prior to moving into this part of the Capitol, the federal government operated first in New York City, then in Philadelphia. Throughout that time, progress was on-going toward making Washington, D. C. the permanent home of the federal government.

That effort began in 1790 when Congress passed a bill authorizing George Washington to choose a site for the Capital City somewhere along the Potomac River. In early 1791, Washington appointed surveyors to begin their work, and by the end of that year, they had completed plans for the city. In 1792, those plans were publicly unveiled and work was begun on the White House. The next year, 1793, construction began on the Capitol. Seven years later, in late 1800, the White House, the Capitol, the Treasury, and other buildings were complete enough that business could be conducted in them, and this was when Congress first moved into the Capitol as its permanent home.

This second plaque in the Small Senate Rotunda notes that on November 22nd, President John Adams delivered the first Presidential speech ever given in this building – a speech given to the first joint-session of Congress assembled in the original Senate Chamber. His speech was quite short, but in it, President John Adams offered his prayer for this city. According to the *Records of Congress*, John Adams prayed:

May this territory [Washington, D.C.] be the residence of virtue and happiness! In this city, may that piety and virtue, that wisdom and magnanimity, that constancy and self-government which adorned the great character whose name it bears, be forever held in veneration! Here and throughout our country, may simple manners, pure morals, and true religion flourish forever! [75]

JOHN ADAMS

This is quite a prayer for Washington, D. C. – and for the nation – and it was a prayer which occurred in the room immediately behind the plaque – the original Senate Chamber (now called the Old Supreme Court Chamber).

Another item of significance connected with this part of the Capitol is one of the first official acts of Congress. This occurred when our Founders moved into and first occupied this room and the adjoining chamber, and this action is recorded in the Annals of Congress.

The records of Congress are required by the constitutional mandate of Article I, Section 5, ¶ 3, which requires that written records be kept of the proceedings in Congress. The Founders required this because they wanted government open, accessible, and accountable to the people.

With the congressional records, citizens, at any time, may read what our elected officials are doing and saying – or not doing and not saying – and then hold them accountable. Every debate and every vote which has taken place in Congress from 1774 to the present is recorded in these public records. And it is because of these records that we know exactly what happened when Congress moved into this building.

According to the records for late November of 1800, Congress spent the first few weeks organizing the rooms, the committees, their loca-

THE RECORDS OF CONGRESS
COMMENCE IN 1774

tions, etc. Then, on December 4, 1800, Congress made an interesting decision: Congress decided that the Capitol building would also serve as a church building! [76]

The use of this building as a church building is confirmed not only by the records of Congress but also by the diaries of those who served in Congress at the time. For

> DECEMBER, 1800.   *Reporting the Debates.*
>
> tory understanding of the state of the Treasury, since the appointment of the Secretary.
> The motion was agreed to.
>
> ---
>
> WEDNESDAY, December 3.
> *Ordered,* That the report of the Committee of Claims on the petition of Oliver Pollock, made the eighteenth of April last, together with his letter presented the twenty-eighth ultimo, be referred to the Committee of Claims.
>
> ---
>
> THURSDAY, December 4.
> Another member, to wit: SAMUEL GOODE, from Virginia, appeared, and took his seat in the House.
> The SPEAKER informed the House that the Chaplains had proposed, if agreeable to the House, to hold Divine service every Sunday in their Chamber.
>
> REPORTING THE DEBATES.

RECORDS OF CONGRESS REPORTING THE DECISION
TO USE THE HOUSE AS A CHURCH

example, while John Quincy Adams was a U. S. Senator, he recorded in his diary for October 30, 1803:

JOHN QUINCY ADAMS

> Attended public service at the Capitol where Mr. Ratoon, an Episcopalian clergyman from Baltimore, preached a sermon. [77]

The week before, he had written:

> [R]eligious service is usually performed on Sundays at the Treasury office and at the Capitol. I went both forenoon and afternoon to the Treasury. [78]

Very few citizens realize that the Capitol building – as well as other government buildings – served as church buildings, but such was the case!

THE OLD SUPREME COURT CHAMBER
(THE ORIGINAL SENATE CHAMBER)

Except for a short period for remodeling, the Senate met in its original chamber (now the Old Supreme Court Chamber) until 1810, when it moved directly upstairs into its second home. Those second quarters, located above the small rotunda with the plaques, are today called the Old Senate Chamber. The Senate remained in that chamber from 1810 until 1859, when it moved into the chamber that it currently occupies. (As already noted, a number of Senators who served in the Old Senate Chamber – e.g., Daniel Webster – were strong men of faith.)

Having investigated the three locations in the Capitol where the Senate met, it is interesting to note some of the locations where the Supreme Court met, because the locations of the Senate and the Supreme Court are directly linked. Significantly, the locations in the Capitol in which the Court met during its first century-and-a-half form a potent commentary on the Founders' views of the power and reach of the Court.

The Founders made remarkably elaborate plans for the city of Washington, D. C. The streets were laid out alphabetically and numerically; and the system was so logical that even today it is easy to find any location in that huge city simply by its address. Our Founders

EARLY CITY PLAN FOR WASHINGTON, D. C.

planned for traffic flow; they anticipated growth; and they made farsighted preparations for the President and the Congress, providing buildings and support services for both. Yet, with all their elaborate preparations, they did *not* provide a separate building for the U. S. Supreme Court. This was not an oversight on their part; the Supreme Court was intended to meet inside the Capitol.

In its first ten years inside the Capitol, the Court bounced around from location to location – from various committee rooms to library rooms to whatever was available. Then, in 1810, when the Senate left its original chamber and moved directly upstairs to what is now called the Old Senate Chamber, the Supreme Court inherited the vacated downstairs Senate chamber.

It was in that room – the basement of the Old Senate Chamber – that the Supreme Court found its first permanent home and the location that it kept for the next 50 years. Then, when the Senate vacated its second home in the Old Senate Chamber and moved into its third and current home, the Supreme Court moved upstairs to possess the again vacated Senate Chamber.

That the Supreme Court had no building of its own was intentional; it reflected the Founders' design that the Court should have no major role in shaping policy in the nation. Simply look at the Constitution for proof: Article I deals with the powers of the Congress; Article II with the powers of the President, and Article III with the powers of the Supreme Court. Article I is by far the longest of those three articles, and Article III is obviously the shortest.

Even though the Founders believed that a Supreme Court was important, it was so insignificant in the overall view of government, that John Jay, the original Chief Justice of the Supreme Court, retired from his position after only six years because, as he observed, the Supreme Court would never amount to anything much. [79] In fact, for the first 10 years of its existence, the entire Supreme Court term lasted less than two weeks each year; and for the next fifty years, the Court still met for only six to eight weeks a year. [80]

It was not until 1935 – nearly a century-and-a-half after the Founders had written the Constitution – that a separate building was built behind the Capitol to house the Supreme Court, the home it occupies today. And it was not until two decades after this, in the late 1950s, that the Supreme Court, under the guidance of its activist Chief Justice, Earl Warren, first began to meet for nearly nine months [81] out of each year – a practice which still continues today.

Yet, despite the Court's original lack of stature, there were several interesting practices of the Court which contribute much to our rich spiritual heritage. One of those practices was instituted by the first Justices on the Court.

There were six original Justices appointed to the Supreme Court by President George Washington. They included its Chief Justice, John Jay, an author of *The Federalist Papers;* three signers of the Constitution: James Wilson, John Blair, and John Rutledge (who later became the Court's second Chief Justice); and James Iredell and William Cushing (who helped secure the ratification of the Constitution).

THE

FEDERALIST,

ON THE NEW CONSTITUTION;

WRITTEN IN 1788,

BY MR. HAMILTON, MR. JAY, AND MR. MADISON

A NEW EDITION,

WITH THE NAMES AND PORTRAITS OF THE SEVERAL WRITERS.

PHILADELPHIA:
PUBLISHED BY BENJAMIN WARNER, NO. 147, MARKET STREET
AND SOLD AT HIS STORES, RICHMOND, VIRGINIA;
AND CHARLESTON, SOUTH CAROLINA.

THE FEDERALIST PAPERS

In its first years, the Supreme Court functioned much like the old circuit courts; it traveled from place to place across America to hear cases and to convene grand juries. One of the practices of the Court – a practice conducted under these original Justices – was the regular offering of prayers in the Courtroom. [82]

According to the records of the Supreme Court as well as the newspapers of the day, juries in the Supreme Court did not begin their work until after a minister had come into the Courtroom and prayed – for the Court, the jurors, and their deliberations! In fact, a newspaper account in the *Columbian Centinel* of May 16, 1792, reports very simply:

> [O]n Monday, Chief Justice [John] Jay gave a charge to the Grand Jury, replete with his usual perspicuity and elegance. The prayer was made by the Rev. Dr. Parker. His Excellency, the Vice-President of the United States [John Adams], was in Court. [83]

Our Founding Fathers never saw such practices as a problem, for they never envisioned any hostility toward religion or any exclusion of religious faith or practice from public life. This was especially true when it came to religion and the law. Explicit proof of this is offered by one of the Court's original members – Justice James Wilson.

JAMES WILSON AT THE
SIGNING OF THE DECLARATION

JAMES WILSON AT THE
SIGNING OF THE CONSTITUTION

Before becoming a member of the Supreme Court, Wilson had signed both the Declaration of Independence and the Constitution (one of only six Founders to hold that distinction). At the Constitutional Convention, Wilson had been its second most-active member, speaking on the floor of the Convention 168 times.

James Wilson is credited with starting the first organized legal training in America for law students. [84] He wrote several legal works, including a 1792 *Commentary on the Constitution of the United States of America,* and a three-volume set of legal lectures, delivered to law students while Wilson was sitting as a Justice on the Court. Notice what Justice Wilson taught his students about the relationship between law and religion:

[I]t should always be remembered that this law, ... made for men or for nations, flows from the same Divine source: it is the law of God. ... What we do, indeed, must be founded on what He has done; and the deficiencies of our laws must be supplied by the perfections of His. Human law must rest its authority, ultimately, upon the authority of that law which is Divine. ... We now see the deep and the solid foundations of human law. ... From this short, but plain and, I hope, just statement of things, we perceive a principle of connection between all the learned professions; but

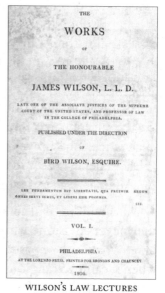

WILSON'S LAW LECTURES

especially between the two last mentioned [the profession of Divinity and the profession of law]. Far from being rivals or enemies, religion and law are twin sisters, friends, and mutual assistants. Indeed, these two sciences run into each other. [85]

---

120   LECTURES ON LAW.

Now that we have stated and answered the first question ; let us proceed to the consideration of the second—how shall we, in particular instances, learn the dictates of our duty, and make, with accuracy, the proper distinction between right and wrong; in other words, how shall we, in particular cases, discover the will of God? We discover it by our conscience, by our reason, and by the Holy Scriptures. The law of nature and the law of revelation are both divine : they flow, though in different channels, from the same adorable source. It is, indeed, preposterous to separate them from each other. The object of both is—to discover the will of God—and both are necessary for the accomplishment of that end.

ANOTHER OF JUSTICE WILSON'S LECTURES ON RELIGION AND LAW

Founding Father and Supreme Court Justice James Wilson, a leading figure in the development of American constitutional law, believed – and taught – that all good civil law must embrace and flow from God's law.

Placed on four pillars around the back of the Old Supreme Court Chamber are four busts – those of John Jay, the first Chief Justice of the United States Supreme Court; John Rutledge, the Court's second Chief Justice; Oliver Ellsworth, its third Chief Justice; and John Marshall, the fourth Chief Justice.

THE COURT'S FIRST CHIEF JUSTICES: JOHN JAY (TOP LEFT), JOHN RUTLEDGE (TOP RIGHT)
OLIVER ELLSWORTH (LOWER LEFT), AND JOHN MARSHALL (LOWER RIGHT)

John Jay, as the Court's first Chief Justice, was, along with James
Wilson, an original member of the Supreme Court. You may recall
that John Jay was a founding vice-president of the American Bible
Society. Five years after he helped found that organization, he be-
came its second president upon the death of its original president,
Elias Boudinot.

The annual speeches John Jay delivered to the American Bible
Society as its president are powerful declarations of his own beliefs

about the efficacy of the Bible. For example, in one of those speeches, Chief Justice John Jay declared:

> By conveying the Bible to people . . . we certainly do them a most interesting act of kindness. We thereby enable them to learn that man was originally created and placed in a state of happiness, but, becoming disobedient, was subjected to the degradation and evils which he and his posterity have since experienced. The Bible will also inform them that our gracious Creator has provided for us a Redeemer in whom all the nations of the earth should be blessed − that this Redeemer has made atonement "for the sins of the whole world," and thereby reconciling the Divine justice with the Divine mercy, has opened a way for our redemption and salvation; and that these inestimable benefits are of the free gift and grace of God, not of our deserving, nor in our power to deserve. The Bible will also [encourage] them with many explicit and consoling assurances of the Divine mercy to our fallen race, and with repeated invitations to accept the offers of pardon and reconciliation. . . . They, therefore, who enlist in His service, have the highest encouragement to fulfil the duties assigned to their respective stations; for most certain it is, that those of His followers who [participate in] His conquests will also participate in the transcendent glories and blessings of His Triumph. [86]

BIBLE SOCIETY DOCUMENT
SIGNED BY JOHN JAY

Under the leadership of its president, John Jay − a Founding Father and the original Chief Justice of the U. S. Supreme Court − tens and thousands of Bibles were printed and distributed across America by the American Bible Society.

Oliver Ellsworth, the Court's third Chief Justice, was a member of the Continental Congress during the American Revolution as well as a member of the Convention that wrote the Constitution. Like the other Founding Fathers, he, too, held strong convictions about religion in public life. For example, in the *Connecticut Courant* of June 7, 1802, Chief Justice Ellsworth declared:

> [T]he primary objects of government, are the peace, order and prosperity of society. . . . To the promotion of these objects, particularly in a republican government, good morals are essential. Institutions for the promotion of good morals are, therefore, objects of legislative provision and support:
>
>
>
> and among these . . . religious institutions are eminently useful and important. . . . [T]he legislature, charged with the great interests of the community, may, and ought to countenance, aid and protect religious institutions – institutions wisely calculated to direct men to the performance of all the duties arising from their
>
> CHIEF JUSTICE OLIVER ELLSWORTH   connection with each other, and
> to prevent or repress those evils which flow from unrestrained passion. . . . [T]he legislature may aid the maintenance of [Christianity], whose benign influence on morals is universally acknowledged. It may be added that this principle has been long recognized, and is too intimately connected with the peace, order and happiness of the state to be abandoned. [87]

This Chief Justice of the United States Supreme Court declared that it was ***proper*** for the State to aid, encourage, and protect religion!

Another Supreme Court Justice who adds to the rich spiritual heritage of the Old Supreme Court Chamber is Joseph Story. Story was truly a son of the American Revolution, for his father had been one of the so-called "Indians" who conducted the Boston Tea Party. Joseph Story became a U. S. Congressman under President Thomas Jefferson. President James Madison appointed him to the Supreme Court to replace the retiring William Cushing, one of the Court's original six Justices. Joseph Story, at age 32, was the youngest Justice ever appointed to the Court.

JUSTICE JOSEPH STORY

Justice Story's accomplishments while on the Court are numerous: he founded Harvard Law School, wrote many legal texts now considered classics, and in his 34 years on the Court, he wrote 286 opinions – 94 percent of which were accepted as the majority decision of the Court. [88] Justice Story clearly is one of the more notable individuals to serve in the Old Supreme Court Chamber.

While there was a period in Justice Story's life in which he attached himself to the Unitarians, and even served as President of the American Unitarian Association, he later declared his regret for those beliefs by which at one time he had questioned Christianity. He lamented:

> It has been my misfortune . . . to have once entertained doubts respecting Christianity. This has ever been viewed by me as an unfortunate circumstance, to remove which, I have labored and read with assiduous attention all of the arguments of its proof. [89]

Justice Story became committed to the principles of Christianity. Throughout his lengthy legal career, he consistently expressed his strong beliefs about the importance of Christianity to civil government and his conviction that American law and legal practices must never be separated from Christian principles. As he explained:

> One of the beautiful boasts of our municipal jurisprudence is that Christianity is a part of the Common Law. . . . There never

has been a period in which the Common Law did not recognize Christianity as lying at its foundations. . . . [The law] pronounces illegal every contract offensive to [Christianity's] morals. It recognizes with profound humility [Christianity's] holidays and festivals, and obeys them [even to the point of suspending all government functions on those days]. It still attaches to persons believing in [Christianity's] Divine authority the highest degree of competency as witnesses. [90]

Some of Justice Story's most famous and authoritative legal writings were his 1833 works expounding the Constitution of the United States. Notice what this distinguished Supreme Court Justice said about Christianity and the Constitution – including the fact that the First Amendment was never intended to separate Christianity from civil government or from civil society:

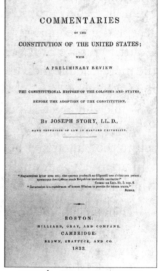

STORY'S 1833 *COMMENTARIES*

The first [amendment] is, "Congress shall make no law respecting an establishment of religion, or prohibiting the free exercise thereof. . . ." . . . We are not to attribute this prohibition of a national religious establishment to an indifference to religion in general, and especially to Christianity, which none could hold in more reverence than the framers of the Constitution. . . . Indeed, the right of a society or government to [participate] in matters of religion will hardly be contested by any persons who believe that piety, religion, and morality are intimately connected with the well being of the state and indispensable to the administrations of civil justice. The promulgation of the great doctrines of religion – the being, and attributes, and providence of one Almighty God; the responsibility to Him for all our actions, founded upon moral accountability; a future state of rewards and punishments; the cultivation of all the personal, social, and benevolent virtues – these never can be a matter of indifference in any well-ordered community. It is, indeed, difficult to conceive how any civilized society can well exist without them. And, at all events, it is impossible for those who believe in the truth of Christianity as a Divine revelation to doubt that it is the especial duty of government to foster and encourage it among all the citizens and subjects. . . . [A]t the time of the adoption of the Constitution and of the [First] amendment to it . . . the general, if not the universal, sentiment in America was, that Christianity ought to receive encouragement from the State. . . . An attempt to level all religions, and to make it a matter of state policy to hold all in utter indifference, would have created universal disapprobation, if not universal indignation. [91]

Joseph Story believed that it was proper to encourage Christianity in the government sphere and in the public arena. He even announced that he would not support anyone who attempted to weaken or remove Christianity's influence from society. He declared:

I verily believe Christianity necessary to the support of civil society, and shall ever attend to its institutions and acknowledge its precepts as the pure and natural sources of private and social happiness. The man who could subvert its influence will *never* receive [approval] from me. [92] (emphasis added)

Strong sentiments from Justice Joseph Story, who sat at bench in the Old Supreme Court Chamber and who today is still called "A Father of American Jurisprudence."

Many important Justices have occupied the Old Supreme Court Chamber and filled its chairs; many important attorneys have argued their cases within that chamber; and many important decisions have been handed down in that room of the Capitol. Two of those cases are worth noting – both of which occurred while Justice Story sat at bench.

One occurred in 1841 and dealt with the Spanish slave-trading ship *Amistad*. Following the ship's journey to Africa to capture slaves, the enslaved Africans revolted in defense of their own liberty, seized control of the *Amistad*, and killed the Captain and first mate. However, not knowing how to navigate the ship they now possessed, they forced two surviving Spaniards to sail them back to Africa.

The Spaniards deceptively sailed the ship to America while convincing the Africans that they were returning to Africa. When the Africans finally disembarked, they found themselves not in Africa but in Connecticut. The two Spaniards then filed charges in American courts against the now free Africans, seeking their return to slavery.

The case [93] proceeded through the legal system and an elderly John Quincy Adams was engaged to argue this case before the Supreme Court. Standing firmly on the principles set forth in the Declaration of Independence, former President John Quincy Adams, now a member of Congress, eloquently – and successfully – argued for the freedom of the Africans.

At the end of that case, in what became his last words ever spoken before the Supreme Court, Adams stood in the Old Supreme Court Chamber, reminisced about the changes he had seen during his long life, and then closed by offering his heart's prayer for each Justice then sitting on the bench. He told the Court:

> May it please your Honors, on the 7th of February, 1804, now more than thirty-seven years past, my name was entered and yet stands recorded ... as one of the Attorneys and Counsellors of this Court. Five years later ... I appeared for the last time before this Court, ... [for v]ery shortly afterwards, I was called to the discharge of other duties – first in distant lands, and in later years, within our own country, but in different departments of her government. Little did I imagine that I should ever again be required to claim the right of appearing in the capacity of an officer of this Court; yet such has been the dictate of my destiny. . . . I stand before the same Court, but not before the same judges. . . . As I cast my eyes along those seats of honor

and of public trust, now occupied by you, they seek in vain for one of those honored and honorable persons whose indulgence listened then to my voice. Marshall – Cushing – Chase – Washington – Johnson – Livingston – Todd – Where are they?. . . Where are they all? Gone! Gone! All gone! . . . I humbly

hope, and fondly trust, that they have gone to receive the rewards of blessedness on high. In taking, then, my final leave of . . . this honorable Court, I can only [offer] a fervent [prayer] to Heaven that every member of [this Court] may go to his final account with as little of earthly frailty to answer for as [possible] . . . and that you may, every one [of you], after the close of a long and virtuous

JOHN QUINCY ADAMS

career in this world, be received at the portals of [Heaven] with the approving sentence – "Well done, good and faithful servant; enter thou into the joy of the Lord." [94]

John Quincy Adams' final case before the Court closed with his fervent prayer that everyone then seated on the Court might enter Heaven under the blessed approval of God Almighty. A powerful prayer which occurred in this room of the Capitol from a powerful Christian statesmen!

Another significant case was decided three years later in 1844, a case called *Vidal v. Girard's Executors*. [95] That case involved Stephen Girard's personal will in which he left seven million dollars to the city of Philadelphia. Two issues were raised in the case. The first related to the heirs: could an individual leave his estate to the government rather than to his heirs? The second related to the establishment of a school. The will required that part of the money should fund a public school for the benefit of orphans and needy children, but that ministers be prohibited from serving on the faculty of the school. This was perceived to be an attempt to prohibit religious instruction for the students, and it was questioned whether any school supported in whole or in part by the government could adopt such a policy. Daniel Webster was called in to argue the case before the Court, and he argued it in the Old Supreme Court Chamber.

THE OLD SUPREME COURT CHAMBER

Today, when an argument is heard before the Supreme Court, the attorney from each side is given thirty minutes. Daniel Webster, however, spent three days arguing his side of the case!

Webster first argued that an individual could not leave his estate to a city government, and he then argued that no government-supported school could ban the teaching of religion to students by banning ministers from the faculty. This second part of his argument was promptly printed and publicly distributed in a booklet: *Mr. Webster's Speech in Defence of the Christian Ministry, and in Favor of the Religious Instruction of the Young. Delivered in the Supreme Court of the United States, February 10, 1844, in the Case of Stephen Girard's Will.*

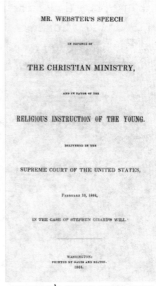

MR. WEBSTER'S SPEECH

IN DEFENCE OF

THE CHRISTIAN MINISTRY,

AND IN FAVOR OF THE

RELIGIOUS INSTRUCTION OF THE YOUNG.

DELIVERED IN THE

SUPREME COURT OF THE UNITED STATES,

FEBRUARY 10, 1844,

IN THE CASE OF STEPHEN GIRARD'S WILL.

WASHINGTON:
PRINTED BY GALES AND SEATON.
1844.

WEBSTER'S COURT ARGUMENTS

When the Court delivered its decision, it was unanimous; and not surprisingly, the decision was written by Justice Joseph Story. The Court first ruled that an individual could leave an estate to a city, and the Court then ruled that while a school might possibly exclude the presence of ministers, such a decision did not mean that it was prohibiting Christianity. Indeed, the Court felt it important that religious teachings be provided to students in any government-supported school. The court explained:

> Why may not the Bible, and especially the New Testament . . . be read and taught as a divine revelation in the [school] – its general precepts expounded, its evidences explained, and its glorious principles of morality inculcated? . . . Where can the purest principles of morality be learned so clearly or so perfectly as from the New Testament? Where are benevolence, the love of truth, sobriety and industry, so powerfully and irresistibly inculcated as in the Sacred Volume? [96]

This unanimous decision on religion in schools, delivered by the Supreme Court in the Old Chamber, is a far cry from the position held by the Supreme Court today.

Perhaps the sculpture engraved in the wall at the back of the Old Supreme Court Chamber most accurately indicates how the earlier Justices viewed their task. That engraved sculpture – directly fronting the Justices as they sat at bench – is of Lady Justice looking to an angel of God who is holding the Constitution of the United States. Indeed, our Founding Fathers and early Justices truly considered upholding the Constitution as a *sacred* trust, delivered to them from God.

ENGRAVED SCULPTURE AT THE BACK OF THE OLD SUPREME COURT CHAMBER

The more one learns of the Capitol building – of how religion was openly embraced and practiced here – of how strongly and how openly religious our Founding Fathers and early leaders were – of how many artifacts, paintings, statues, and rooms in the Capitol openly honor religious faith – the more illogical it is to assert that America's history requires her to maintain a secular, religion-free government and public society. Such simply is not the case.

The Capitol building is filled with stories and accounts like those described here. And although we have covered much, we have only touched the tip of the proverbial iceberg. Yet, even this small

amount affirms that there truly is a deep and rich spiritual heritage in the Capitol building – as there is in so many of the monuments and structures throughout this great city. I encourage you to visit Washington, D. C., and especially to come see for yourself the wonderful heritage to be found in the Capitol of the United States! ∎

CONGRESSIONAL MOTTO LOCATED IN THE CHAMBERS OF
CONGRESS AS WELL AS IN THE CONGRESSIONAL OFFICE BUILDINGS

"Righteousness exalteth a nation." PROVERBS 14:34A

"Blessed is the nation whose God is the Lord." PSALMS 33:12A

• • • •

FIRST PRAYER IN CONGRESS, 1774

Appendix A: Map of the Capitol

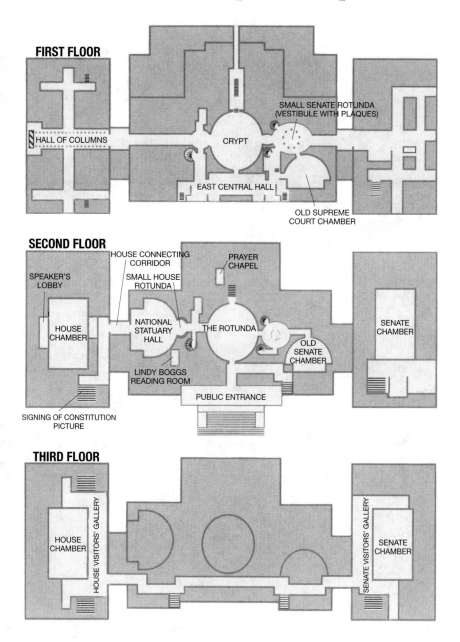

FIRST FLOOR

HALL OF COLUMNS

CRYPT

SMALL SENATE ROTUNDA
(VESTIBULE WITH PLAQUES)

EAST CENTRAL HALL

OLD SUPREME
COURT CHAMBER

SECOND FLOOR

HOUSE CONNECTING
CORRIDOR

PRAYER
CHAPEL

SPEAKER'S
LOBBY

SMALL HOUSE
ROTUNDA

HOUSE
CHAMBER

NATIONAL
STATUARY
HALL

THE ROTUNDA

SENATE
CHAMBER

OLD
SENATE
CHAMBER

LINDY BOGGS
READING ROOM

SIGNING OF CONSTITUTION
PICTURE

PUBLIC ENTRANCE

THIRD FLOOR

HOUSE
CHAMBER

HOUSE VISITORS' GALLERY

SENATE VISITORS' GALLERY

SENATE
CHAMBER

Appendix B: Endnotes

1. *The Encyclopedia Britannica*, 11th ed., s.v. "Bible, English."
2. William Bradford, *History of Plymouth Plantation* (Boston: Little, Brown, and Company, 1856), p. 6.
3. Bradford, *History*, pp. 134-136.
4. *The Encyclopedia Britannica*, 11th ed., s.v. "Bible, English."
5. *The Encyclopedia Britannica*, 11th ed., s.v. "Bible, English."
6. George Bancroft, *History of the United States, From the Discovery of the American Continent* (Boston: Little, Brown, and Company, 1859), p. 266; see also *The Holy Bible, As Printed by Robert Aitken and Approved & Recommended by the Congress of the United States of America in 1782* (New York: Arno Press, 1968), preface.
7. Gordon Wood, "The Radical Revolution: An Interview with Gordon Wood," interview by Fredric Smoler, *American Heritage*, December, 1992, p. 52.
8. Steven Morris, "America's Unchristian Beginnings," *The Los Angeles Times*, August 3, 1995, p. B-9. This article was picked up on wire services and appeared in newspapers across the nation.
9. Michael A. Macdonald, "Founding Fathers Weren't Devout," *The Charlotte Observer*, Friday, January 15, 1993, p. 7A.
10. Isaac Kramnick and R. Laurence Moore, *The Godless Constitution, The Case Against Religious Correctness* (New York: W. W. Norton & Company, 1996).
11. B. J. Lossing, *Biographical Sketches of the Signers of the Declaration of American Independence* (New York: George F. Cooledge & Brother, 1848).
12. *The Holy Bible, Containing the Old and New Testaments* (Trenton: Isaac Collins, 1791), preface, "To The Reader," by John Witherspoon.
13. Charles Carroll to Charles W. Wharton, Esq., September 27, 1825, from an original letter in our possession.
14. Kate Mason Rowland, *The Life of Charles Carroll of Carrollton* (New York: Knickerbocker Press, 1898), Vol. II, pp. 328-329, 400, from his will, September 2, 1825.
15. L. H. Butterfield, "The Reputation of Benjamin Rush," *Pennsylvania History*, January 1950, Vol. XVII, No. 1, p. 9, John Adams to Richard Rush, May 5, 1813; see also *Delaplaine's Repository of the Lives and Portraits of Distinguished American Characters* (Philadelphia, 1815-1816), Vol. I, p. 42.
16. *An Address of the Bible Society Established at Philadelphia to the Public* (Philadelphia: Fry and Kammerer, 1809), p. 15.
17. *Debates and Proceedings in the Congress of the United States* (Washington, DC: Gales and Seaton, 1853), p. 1325, Twelfth Congress, 2nd Session, "An Act for the Relief of the Bible Society of Philadelphia," February 2, 1813.
18. *Dictionary of American History*, s.v. "Prison-ships" and s.v. "Wars: Loss of Life in Major United States Wars"; see also *Letters of Delegates to Congress, 1774-1789*, Paul H. Smith, editor (Washington, DC: Library of Congress, 1995), Vol. 22, p. 442, Joseph Platt Cooke to Amos Cooke, June 8, 1785.
19. Will of Richard Stockton, May 20, 1780.
20. A. J. Dallas, *Reports of Cases Ruled and Adjudged in the Courts of Pennsylvania* (Philadelphia: P. Byrne, 1806), p. 39, *Respublica v. John Roberts;* (Pa. Sup. Ct. 1778).

21. William B. Reed, *Life and Correspondence of Joseph Reed* (Philadelphia: Lindsay and Blakiston, 1847), pp. 36-37.

22. John Hancock, *A Proclamation For a Day of Public Thanksgiving* (Boston, 1791), for November 17, 1791.

23. Samuel Adams, *A Proclamation For a Day of Public Fasting, Humiliation and Prayer* (Boston, 1795), for November 19, 1795; see also Samuel Adams, *The Writings of Samuel Adams*, Harry Alonzo Cushing, editor (New York: G. P. Putnam's Sons, 1908), Vol. IV, p. 385, October 14, 1795.

24. Adams, *Writings*, Vol. IV, p. 407, from his proclamation for May 4, 1797.

25. See *Journals of the American Congress from 1774 to 1788* (Washington, DC: Way and Gideon, 1823), for June 12, 1775, March 16, 1776, December 11, 1776, November 1, 1777, March 7, 1778, November 17, 1778, March 20, 1779, October 20, 1779, March 11, 1780, October 18, 1780, March 20, 1781, October 26, 1781, March 19, 1782, October 11, 1782, October 18, 1783.

26. Memorial of Robert Aitken to Congress, January 21, 1781, obtained from the National Archives, Washington, DC; see also *The Holy Bible, as Printed by Robert Aitken*, Introduction.

27. *The New Annual Register or General Repository of History, Politics, and Literature, for the Year 1783* (London: G. Robinson, 1784), p. 143, opening line of final Treaty of Peace.

28. George Washington, *The Last Official Address of His Excellency George Washington to the Legislatures of the United States* (Hartford: Hudson and Goodwin, 1783), p. 12; see also *Annual Register*, p. 150.

29. William M. Thayer, *From Log-Cabin to the White House* (Boston: James H. Earle, 1881), pp. 208-224.

30. James Garfield to Wallace Ford, February 16, 1858, from an original letter in our possession.

31. Paul Wallace, *The Muhlenbergs of Pennsylvania* (Philadelphia: University of Pennsylvainia Press, 1950), p. 121; see also *Dictionary of American Biography*, s.v. "Fredrick Muhlenberg."

32. John Quincy Adams, *Memoirs of John Quincy Adams, Comprising Portions of His Diary from 1795 to 1848*, Charles Francis Adams, editor (Philadelphia: J. B. Lippincott & Co., 1874), Vol. VII, p. 325, August 20, 1827.

33. George Washington, *The Writings of George Washington*, Jared Sparks, editor (Boston: Russell, Shattuck, and Williams, and Hilliard, Gray and Co., 1836), Vol. XI, p. 188, to John Adams, February 20, 1797.

34. John Quincy Adams, *An Oration Delivered Before the Inhabitants of the Town of Newburyport, At Their Request, on the Sixty-First Anniversary of the Declaration of Independence, July 4th, 1837* (Newburyport: Charles Whipple, 1837), pp. 5, 6.

35. Adams, *1837 Oration*, pp. 5, 6.

36. Adams, *1837 Oration*, pp. 5, 6.

37. John Quincy Adams, *Letters of John Quincy Adams, to His Son on the Bible and Its Teachings* (New York: Derby, Miller, & Co., 1848), pp. 10-11.

38. B. F. Tefft, *Webster and His Master-Pieces* (Auburn: Miller, Orton & Mulligan, 1854), Vol. I, p. 496.

39. *Addresses in the Congress of the United States, and Funeral Solemnities on the Death of John Quincy Adams* (Washington, DC: J. and G. S. Gideon, 1848), pp. 3-4.

40. Robert C. Winthrop, *Addresses and Speeches on Various Occasions* (Boston: Little, Brown, and Company, 1852), p. 172, "An Address Delivered at the Annual Meeting of the Massachusetts Bible Society in Boston," May 28, 1849.

41. Ethan Allen, *A Narrative of Colonel Ethan Allen's Captivity* (Burlington: H. Johnson & Co., 1838), pp. 17-18.

42. Irving McKee, *"Ben-Hur" Wallace, The Life of General Lew Wallace* (Berkeley: University of California Press, 1947), p. 167.

43. McKee, *Wallace*, pp. 173-174.

44. Lew Wallace, *The Illustrated Ben-Hur* (New York: Bonanza Books, 1978), from President Garfield to General Wallace, April 19, 1881.

45. Joseph Banvard, *Daniel Webster, His Life and Public Services* (Chicago: Werner Company, 1875), pp. 131-133.

46. Charles Lanman, *The Private Life of Daniel Webster* (New York: Harper & Brothers, 1853), pp. 21-22.

47. Lanman, *Webster*, p. 103.

48. Banvard, *Webster*, pp. 30-31.

49. Daniel Webster, *Mr. Webster's Address at the Laying of the Corner Stone of the Addition to the Capitol, July 4th, 1851* (Washington, DC: Gideon And Co., 1851), p. 23; see also Daniel Webster, *The Works of Daniel Webster* (Boston: Little, Brown & Co., 1853), Vol. II, pp. 614-615.

50. Webster, *Works*, Vol. I, p. 44, from "A Discourse Delivered at Plymouth," December 22, 1820.

51. I. W. Stuart, *Life of Jonathan Trumbull, Sen., Governor of Connecticut* (Hartford: Belknap & Warfield, 1859), p. 605.

52. Lewis Henry Boutell, *The Life of Roger Sherman* (Chicago: A. C. McClurg and Company, 1896), pp. 271-273.

53. E. Edwards Beardsley, *Life and Times of William Samuel Johnson* (Boston: Houghton, Mifflin and Company, 1886), pp. 141-145.

54. Jacob Broom to his son, James, on February 24, 1794, from an original letter in our possession.

55. Alexander Hamilton, *The Works of Alexander Hamilton*, John C. Hamilton, editor (New York: John F. Trow, 1851), from three letters: Vol. VI, p. 453, to James A. Bayard, August 6, 1800; Vol. VI, p. 486, to Oliver Wolcott, Jr., December 16, 1800; and Vol. VI, pp. 499-501, to James A. Bayard, December 27, 1800.

56. Eliphalet Nott, *A Discourse Delivered in the North Dutch Church in the City of Albany, Occasioned by the Ever to be Lamented Death of General Alexander Hamilton, July 29, 1804* (Salem: Joshua Cushing, 1804), pp. 34-35, among statements enclosed with his last will and testament; see also Alexander Hamilton, *The Papers of Alexander Hamilton*, Harold C. Syrett, editor (New York: Columbia University Press, 1977), Vol. XXVI, p. 280, "Statement on Impending Duel with Aaron Burr," June 28, 1804.

57. Nott, *Discourse*, pp. 34-35; see also Hamilton, *Papers*, Vol. XXVI, p. 280, "Statement on Impending Duel with Aaron Burr," June 28, 1804.

58. John M. Mason, *A Collection of the Facts and Documents Relative to the Death of Major General Alexander Hamilton* (New York: Hopkins and Seymour, 1804), p. 53.

59. Mason, *Collection*, pp. 48-50.

60. Hamilton, *Works*, Vol. VI, p. 542, to James A. Bayard, April, 1802; see also Hamilton, *Papers*, Vol. XXV, p. 606, to James A. Bayard, April 16, 1802.

61. *Constitution of the American Bible Society* (New York: American Bible Society, 1816), p. 7; see also Henry Otis Dwight, *The Centennial History of the American Bible Society* (New York: Macmillan Company, 1916), pp. 29-30.

62. *Dictionary of American Biography*, s.v. "James McHenry."

63. Bernard C. Steiner, *One Hundred and Ten Years of Bible Society Work in Maryland* (Maryland Bible Society, 1921), p. 14.

64. George Washington, *Maxims of Washington; Political, Social, Moral and Religious*, John F. Schroeder, editor (New York: D. Appleton and Company, 1855).

65. Washington, *Maxims* (1855), p. 367.

66. Washington, *Maxims* (1855), p. 367.

67. Washington, *Maxims* (1855), p. 367.

68. Washington, *Maxims* (1855), p. 367.

69. Washington, *Maxims* (1855), p. 367.

70. George Washington, *Maxims of George Washington; Political, Military, Social, Moral, and Religious*, John Frederick Schroeder, editor (Mount Vernon, VA: Mount Vernon Ladies' Association, 1989).

71. Washington, *Maxims* (1989), p. 164.

72. "I Smell a Rat!" *World Magazine*, February 14, 1998, p. 17.

73. Washington, *Writings*, pp. 406-407, Nelly Custis to Jared Sparks, February 26, 1833.

74. Washington, *Writings*, Vol, XII, p. 407, from the account of Mr. Robert Lewis [nephew of George Washington], to Jared Sparks; see also Bishop Meade, *Old Churches, Ministers and Families of Virginia* (Philadelphia: J. B. Lippincott Company), p. 492.

75. *Debates and Proceedings*, p. 724, Sixth Congress, November 22, 1800.

76. *Debates and Proceedings*, p. 797, Sixth Congress, December 4, 1800.

77. John Quincy Adams, *Memoirs*, Vol. I, p. 268, October 30, 1803.

78. John Quincy Adams, *Memoirs*, Vol. I, p. 265, October 23, 1803.

79. John Jay, *The Correspondence and Public Papers of John Jay, 1794-1826*, Henry P. Johnston, editor (New York: Burt Franklin, 1890), Vol. IV, p. 285, to President Adams, January 2, 1801.

80. Dates of Supreme Court terms found in the Minutes and the Journal of the Supreme Court, supplied by the Library of the Supreme Court of the United States.

81. Supplied by the Library of the Supreme Court ; see also *An Autobiography of the Supreme Court*, Alan Westin, editor (New York: MacMillan Company, 1964), p. 256.

82. *The Documentary History of the Supreme Court of the United States, 1789-1800*, Maeva Marcus, editor (New York: Columbia University Press, 1988), Vol. II, pp. 192, 276, 412; Vol. III, p. 436.

83. *Columbian Centinel* (Boston), May 16, 1792; see also *Documentary History of the Supreme Court*, Vol. II, p. 276.

84. *Dictionary of American Biography*, s.v. "James Wilson."

85. James Wilson, *The Works of the Honorable James Wilson*, Bird Wilson, editor (Philadelphia: Lorenzo Press, 1804), pp. 104-106.

86. Jay, *Correspondence*, Vol. IV, pp. 494, 498, "Address at the Annual Meeting of the American Bible Society," May 13, 1824.

87. Oliver Ellsworth, "A Report of the Committee . . . To the General Assembly of the State of Connecticut," *The Connecticut Courant* (Hartford), June 7, 1802, p. 3.

88. *Dictionary of American Biography,* s.v. "Joseph Story."

89. Joseph Story, *Life and Letters of Joseph Story,* William W. Story, editor (Boston: Charles C. Little and James Brown, 1851), Vol. I, p. 92, March 24, 1801.

90. Story, *Life and Letters,* Vol. II, pp. 8-9, August 25, 1829.

91. Joseph Story, *A Familiar Exposition of the Constitution of the United States* (New York: Harper & Brothers, 1847), pp. 259-261, §440-§443; see also Joseph Story, *Commentaries on the Constitution of the United States* (Boston: Hilliard, Gray, and Company, 1833), Vol. III, pp. 722-731, §1864-1873.

92. Story, *Life and Letters,* Vol. I, pp. 92-93, March 24, 1801.

93. *United States v. Amistad;* 40 U. S. 518 (1841).

94. *Argument of John Quincy Adams, Before the Supreme Court of the United States, in the case of the United States, Appellants, v. Cinque, and others, Africans, Captured in the Schooner Amistad, By Lieut. Gedney, Delivered on the 24th of February and 1st of March, 1841* (New York: S. W. Benedict, 1841).

95. *Vidal v. Girard's Executors;* 43 U. S. 126 (1844).

96. *Vidal* at 200.

Appendix C: Picture Credits

p. 6 – The Capitol in 1800; LIBRARY OF CONGRESS
p. 6 – The Capitol in 1807; LIBRARY OF CONGRESS
p. 7 – The Capitol in 1814; LIBRARY OF CONGRESS
p. 7 – Design for the Extension of the Capitol; THE ATHENAEUM OF PHILADELPHIA
p. 9 – The Landing of Columbus; COURTESY OF THE ARCHITECT OF THE CAPITOL
p. 9 – Discovery of the Mississippi; COURTESY OF THE ARCHITECT OF THE CAPITOL
p. 10 – The Baptism of Pocahontas; COURTESY OF THE ARCHITECT OF THE CAPITOL
p. 10 – The Embarkation of the Pilgrims; COURTESY OF THE ARCHITECT OF THE CAPITOL
p. 11 – The Declaration of Independence; COURTESY OF THE ARCHITECT OF THE CAPITOL
p. 11 – Surrender of General Burgoyne; COURTESY OF THE ARCHITECT OF THE CAPITOL
p. 12 – The Surrender of Cornwallis at Yorktown; COURTESY OF THE ARCHITECT OF THE CAPITOL
p. 12 – General George Washington Resigning His Commission; COURTESY OF THE ARCHITECT OF THE CAPITOL
p. 18 – Pocahontas; COURTESY OF THE ARCHITECT OF THE CAPITOL
p. 18 – John Trumbull, self-portrait, 1777; BOSTON, MUSEUM OF FINE ARTS
p. 20 – The Signing of the Constitution; COURTESY OF THE ARCHITECT OF THE CAPITOL
p. 21 – George Clinton Statue; COURTESY OF THE ARCHITECT OF THE CAPITOL
p. 21 – William Livingston Statue; COURTESY OF THE ARCHITECT OF THE CAPITOL
p. 25 – Charles Carroll Statue; COURTESY OF THE ARCHITECT OF THE CAPITOL
p. 28 – Prison Ship, Charles Allen Munn Collection; FORDHAM UNIVERSITY LIBRARY
p. 28 – Richard Stockton Statue; COURTESY OF THE ARCHITECT OF THE CAPITOL
p. 30 – John Hancock Statue; COURTESY OF THE ARCHITECT OF THE CAPITOL
p. 32 – Samuel Adams Statue; COURTESY OF THE ARCHITECT OF THE CAPITOL
p. 33 – Robert Aitken; HISTORICAL SOCIETY OF PENNSYLVANIA
p. 35 – President Garfield Statue; COURTESY OF THE ARCHITECT OF THE CAPITOL
p. 36 – John Peter Muhlenberg Statue; COURTESY OF THE ARCHITECT OF THE CAPITOL
p. 38 – Frederick Augustus Muhlenberg; COURTESY OF THE ARCHITECT OF THE CAPITOL
p. 39 – Blackstone Relief; COURTESY OF THE ARCHITECT OF THE CAPITOL
p. 39 – Grotius Relief; COURTESY OF THE ARCHITECT OF THE CAPITOL
p. 39 – Hammurabi Relief; COURTESY OF THE ARCHITECT OF THE CAPITOL
p. 39 – Moses Relief; COURTESY OF THE ARCHITECT OF THE CAPITOL
p. 40 – John Quincy Adams; NATIONAL PARK SERVICE, ADAMS NATIONAL HISTORICAL PARK
p. 44 – John Quincy Adams; METROPOLITAN MUSEUM OF ART
p. 45 – John Quincy Adams; METROPOLITAN MUSEUM OF ART
p. 45 – Couch on which John Quincy Adams died; COURTESY U.S. CAPITOL HISTORICAL SOCIETY
p. 47 – Ethan Allen Statue; COURTESY OF THE ARCHITECT OF THE CAPITOL
p. 49 – The Capture of Fort Ticonderoga; FORT TICONDEROGA MUSEUM
p. 50 – President Grant Statue; COURTESY OF THE ARCHITECT OF THE CAPITOL
p. 50 – General Lew Wallace Statue; COURTESY OF THE ARCHITECT OF THE CAPITOL
p. 51 – Daniel Webster Statue; COURTESY OF THE ARCHITECT OF THE CAPITOL
p. 53 – Daniel Webster in the Old Senate Chamber; LIBRARY OF CONGRESS

Other images, documents, and books owned by Specialty Research Associates, Inc.

Also Available from WallBuilders

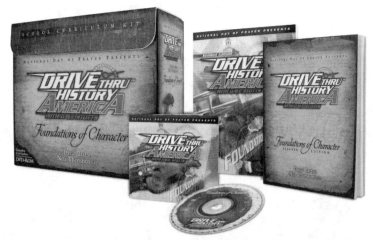

A history curriculum that unabashedly delivers the truth!
Drive Through History America
written by David Barton & presented by award-winning actor Dave Stotts

Visit our website for other great resources!

800-873-2845 • www.wallbuilders.com